"

MAKE A CUSTOMER HAPPY
AND THEY'LL TELL A FRIEND.

MAKE A CUSTOMER ANGRY
AND THEY'LL TELL TEN FRIENDS.

"

The Book of Letters
to
Saint Clinton

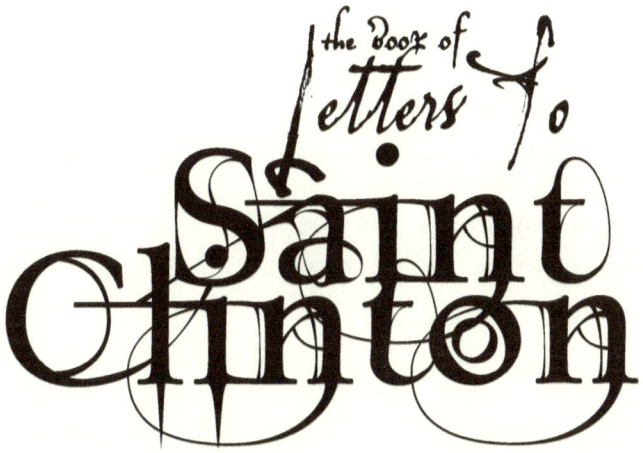

the book of
letters to
Saint Clinton

"Louisville — artist scott ritcher said his depiction of former president clinton as *saint clinton* was meant to be funny and provoke thought, but a catholic priest wasn't amused. the rev. donald hill advised in a letter that any lunch boxes, notebooks or shirts bearing the image are banned from the parish school of st. albert the great catholic church. the clinton portrait was modeled after traditional *sacred heart of jesus* images."

—usa today,
sept. 20, 2004

K Composite
Media

www.kcomposite.com

ALSO BY SCOTT RITCHER:

SLAMDEK A TO Z: THE ILLUSTRATED HISTORY OF LOUISVILLE'S SLAMDEK RECORD COMPANY, 1986-1995 (1996)

K COMPOSITE MAGAZINE: ISSUES 1 TO 5 (2005)

K COMPOSITE MAGAZINE: ISSUES 6 TO 12 (2006)

K COMPOSITE MEDIA
POST OFFICE BOX 43551
LOUISVILLE, KENTUCKY 40253

WWW.KCOMPOSITE.COM

ISBN 978-0-6151-3898-5

LETTERS TO SAINT CLINTON
SECOND EDITION
PRINTED IN THE UNITED STATES

THANK YOU: SARAH BAKER AND RYAN MAGILL

SPECIAL THANKS: SWANSON REED CONTEMPORARY GALLERIES

COVER IMAGE: DETAIL OF "SAINT CLINTON" BY SCOTT RITCHER, © 2003 K COMPOSITE

COMPOSED AND DESIGNED USING APPLE MACINTOSH COMPUTERS LOADED WITH MACROMEDIA FREEHAND AND ADOBE PHOTOSHOP.

SOME NAMES HAVE BEEN CHANGED TO PROTECT PRIVACY.

Introduction
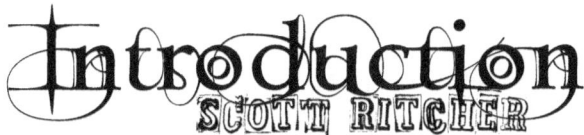
SCOTT RITCHER

"Saint Clinton" was originally created to be added to the Picture Gallery on a news and current events web site I edit called News N Shit (www.newsnshit.com). News N Shit had been around for a little over a year and got an early boost in an MTV News story by Gideon Yago about alternative news and activism sites in the run-up to the invasion of Iraq in 2003.

Most of the other entries in the Picture Gallery were photos I had taken of unusual signs: An electronic display in a Boston subway station that is showing the single word "Rebooting." An Adopt-a-Highway sign in Kentucky with the word "childern" instead of "children." A man standing on the sidewalk in Hollywood with a sign that says, "All religions are fake except Born-Again Christian." A traffic control sign on the Pennsylvania Turnpike displaying the phrase, "Batterys need recharging." A business in Kansas City called Ed's Dainty Corsages, and one in Providence called Bed, Bath & Work Clothes. Part of a map on an information kiosk at the Cleveland airport that says, "Signifies Kiosk You Are At."

Several entries in the News N Shit Picture Gallery were doctored photos or cartoons: A proposition for the design of the new World Trade Center towers, which looked just like the old ones, except they were in the shape of the letters "F.U." A collage of corporate logos that were arranged to form the shape of George

W. Bush's face. Images of U.S. warplanes and aircraft carriers and the slogan, "WWJD?" and Bush quotes such as, "If you want to respond to what has happened in our country, you can do so with prayer, but as importantly, you can do so by loving your neighbor like you'd like to be loved yourself."

Saint Clinton is not a real painting, but actually an electronic file, based on elements from several different images of 18th Century Sacred Heart of Jesus paintings and contemporary White House file photos of President Clinton. I spent a few days working on the image – adding, subtracting and blending colors and elements – to get it to look just right, and I have amended it a few times since to fit different dimensions and configurations. Some versions are smoothed out, while on others the texture of canvas and brush strokes can be seen. I dabbled for a while in trying to replace the flaming heart with a shining presidential seal, but couldn't get it to look right. I reversed the body on the figure purely for aesthetic reasons, so the shadows on the body and robes would match the angle of the shadows on the Clinton images I was working from.

Right off the bat, people seemed to really love Saint Clinton. Perhaps it was the authentic-looking quality of the image. Perhaps it was that we were being led into an unprovoked war and no amount of protest seemed noticed. Maybe it was the economic downturn, rising unemployment, international hatred of our country. Maybe it was just because it looked funny. Perhaps it was the instant irony that Bill Clinton has a reputation as one of the most human public figures of our time. Maybe it was seen as a deliberate smack in the face to Christian conservatism, for whom Jesus is the most loved icon and Clinton is the most despised adversary. It could have been anything. I'm sure the image had a different appeal to everyone who saw it.

All those reasons, I suppose, could also be listed as partial impetus for why I created the image. Primarily, though, I made it because I thought it would be funny.

I have never been a Democrat or a Republican, and until

George W. Bush's presidency I saw both parties as being equally abhorrent and corrupt. Sure, I've voted for members of both parties, but I've rarely been satisfied in knowing that a candidate was the best person for the job.

When I was a candidate for the office of Louisville mayor in 1998, Bill Clinton was in office and embroiled in scandal. I thought exactly what a lot of people thought at the time, that he was an embarrassment to our country. I was among those who felt it was appropriate for him to resign. Now, I feel I couldn't have been more wrong. The only justifiable causes for Clinton's resignation came from his personal indiscretions, which should have remained personal. As James Carville said of the Kenneth Starr investigation, all of us have done stupid things in our lives, but none of us have had eighty million dollars spent by thousands of investigators to find out what those stupid things are. Just like the billions now being spent in Iraq, those millions of dollars should have been spent providing better health and education for the people who paid that money into the system.

Millions of dollars were spent in an effort to demoralize and discredit a man whose failing was that he lied so his wife wouldn't find out he got a blow job. The end result, instead, is that the entire country was exposed to the private business of a married couple's personal problems. Clinton was certainly not the first public official to engage in unusual or extramarital sexual activity, as we know from the affairs of the Kennedy brothers with Marilyn Monroe, or the indiscretions of Eleanor Roosevelt or J. Edgar Hoover.

While I agree that if a military officer or teacher had done the same as Clinton they would have been fired, the difference is that teachers and military officers rarely are the subject of multi-million-dollar investigations. If they were, I feel we'd have an even smaller number of people volunteering to join the military or teach our kids.

If you're offended that your children or grandchildren learned about oral sex from the whole debacle, or learned that it's okay to cheat on your wife, I feel the blame lies more in the hands of Ken Starr and his Republican supporters in Congress whose expensive investigation produced nothing in the way of criminal charges. Rather, it brought private sexual matters into the mainstream media.

When Hillary Clinton spoke of a vast right-wing conspiracy to bring down the down the president, millions – myself included – laughed and thought she was crazy. In retrospect, I wish I had been able to see that where there's smoke there is not necessarily always fire. Sometimes it's just a bunch of assholes with smoke machines.

Two separate, independent investigations into White Water – the June 1994 Pillsbury Report and the 1996 findings of Republican former US Attorney Jay Stevens – both exonerated the Clintons of any criminal wrongdoing.

Late in 2003, I began using the Saint Clinton image on advertisements for the News N Shit site. I printed up a bunch of cards with Saint Clinton on them. At first glance, these cards looked just like the prayer cards depicting individual saints, Jesus or Mary which are handed out at Catholic baptisms, funerals and the like. Rather than the saint's name at the bottom, my cards had a 2-line ad for the web site. I began handing out the Saint Clinton prayer cards at concerts, among friends and leaving them around the city. The reactions I got from these cards were the first personal experiences I had with how powerfully people reacted to the image, and the response was overwhelmingly positive and supportive.

As more and more feedback came back to me about Saint Clinton, people began asking me if they could get other items like posters or stickers. After enough people had asked, in spring 2004, I began offering the image on a variety of products to help support the costs of operating the site. Cafe Press, a California-based company, seemed perfect as the manufacturer and distributor. Cafe Press operates dozens of small and similar online stores. The company offers a range of products on which any of their affiliated merchants/designers can sell their slogans and imagery. So I did all the designs, and now they handle all the credit card processing, manufacturing and fulfillment of the items, then send me a cut of the profit.

In August 2004, in order to draw more attention to the products, I created a new site whose purpose was only to sell and promote Saint Clinton and other related items. The new site, www.SaintClinton.com, is tied to the online stores of some of my other get-rich-slow schemes: News N Shit, K Composite Magazine and Louisville.cc. The range of products being offered include coffee cups and blank journals emblazoned with Victor Hammer's now-retired City of Louisville 1778 seal; Saint Clinton lunch boxes and posters; and a variety of bumper stickers with ridiculous slogans such as "Ask me about my hostages," "USA! We're #2!" and "I Love Abortion."

With the launch of SaintClinton.com, I issued an electronic press announcement to a variety of print and broadcast news media in early September. For a couple weeks thereafter, it was pretty quiet. That is, I felt like I had wasted my time and money in setting up the new site and sending out the PR statement.

Around mid-September, David Walton from the Courier-Journal called me, interested in adding Saint Clinton to his daily column, The Buzz. I was excited about that, and surprised that out of all the releases I had sent out, the first interest was local. David said someone else at the Courier had forwarded it to him and that it had been around the office for a while.

The next day, September 16, Saint Clinton appeared in full color at the top left corner of the front of the Features section in The Buzz. The article was just four paragraphs – short and sweet – it listed the site address, mentioned a few of the products available and noted the earlier MTV News site coverage.

My phone started ringing almost immediately that morning. That's also when the local backlash started. That afternoon I appeared on WHAS Radio during the Terry Meiners and Company show. As soon as I was off the air, Terry started getting emails

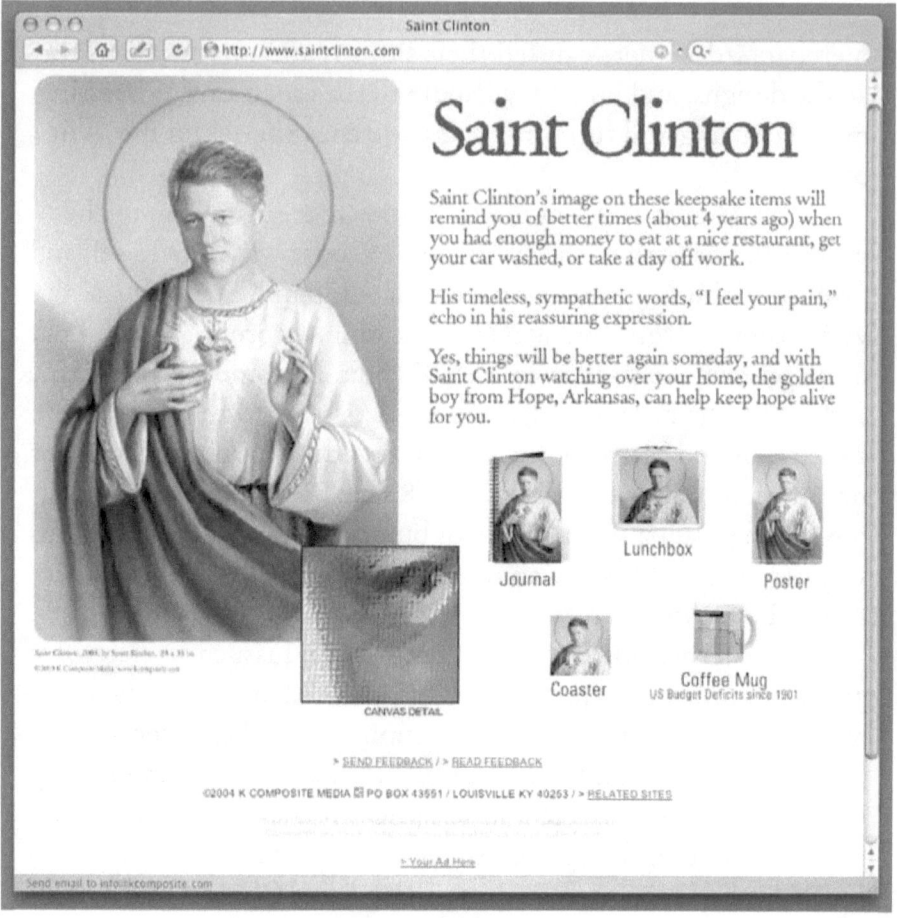

FIG. 1: www.SaintClinton.com

"Saint Clinton's image on these keepsake items will remind you of better times (about 4 years ago) when you had enough money to eat at a nice restaurant, get your car washed, or take a day off work.

"His timeless, sympathetic words, 'I feel your pain,' echo in his reassuring expression.

"Yes, things will be better again someday, and with Saint Clinton watching over your home, the golden boy from Hope, Arkansas, can help keep hope alive for you."

from disgusted listeners.

The next evening's 5:30 news on CBS affiliate WLKY-TV 32 began with Saint Clinton as the "Big Story," as a priest at St. Albert the Great parish school had sent a note home with parents warning that Saint Clinton was blasphemous and banned from the school's campus. Parents were informed that any Saint Clinton lunch boxes or other items students brought to school would be confiscated. When NewsChannel 32 reporter Abby Miller asked me what I thought about that on camera, all I could do was laugh. Maybe that sent the wrong message, but that's how I felt about it. I told Abby I thought that if the school was instilling the proper values in the students, they wouldn't have to ban anything because the kids would know what was inappropriate. Furthermore, confiscating someone else's property, I didn't feel, was a very Christian thing to do.

The next few weeks brought on a tidal wave of letters and emails from self-proclaimed Christians who acted in ridiculously un-Christian ways.

The Courier-Journal ran a second piece about Saint Clinton two days later, but this time it was a news piece. That article – with the headline "School bans 'saintly' Clinton" – was distributed on the Associated Press wire and showed up in nearly a dozen newspapers and broadcast outlets across the country during the following week, including the Cincinnati Enquirer, WBFF-TV Fox 45 in Baltimore and, most notably, USA Today on September 20.

Along with the press coverage also came an immeasurably expansive distribution of the story and image on Web sites, blogs and discussion boards, which ranged in themes and opinions as varied as Christian conservative, comical, artistic, political, pro-life, anti-Clinton, free speech, hate crimes, First Amendment, lapsed Catholics, you name it.

Catholics and Christians were enraged. They each had their own reasons why, and they all felt like telling me about it. Some of the messages I was getting were so outrageous that I began posting them – positive and negative – on a new Feedback page at SaintClinton.com. As upset and entertained people began emailing the URL to each other, those people got even more upset or entertained when they discovered the other items I was selling. One line of particular interest to the outraged was the baby bibs, infant tees and women's thongs that carry the slogan "I love abortion."

More articles continued to surface in Britain's The Guardian, Norway's Startsiden Magazine, the US pro-life outlet Life News, NU in Holland, the Lexington Herald Leader and World Net Daily.

The World Net Daily article included several comments that had been posted on SaintClinton.com, as well as a somewhat lengthy response to critics that I posted on the Amy Welborn Open Book religious site. I naievly thought that this diatribe of mine would help people understand where I was coming from.

When I made the piece, I felt like some people wouldn't like it, but I really had no idea of the outrageous ways that people would respond to it. I have been more than a little surprised by the some of the commentary I've heard and read, and many of the emails I've received from people who call themselves Christians, and yet behave in such a very un-Christian manner.

The basis of this work and most of the other work I've done on the saintclinton.com site, including the "I love abortion" items is intended to be humorous and ironic. I feel silly that I even have to say that. People are so defensive over everything these days, and so eager to fight at the smallest suggestion of conflicting ideals. Honestly, I cannot imagine that anyone actually loves abortion. Seriously, people. I would be shocked if even a single abortion practitioner loves what he does for a living.

So much of American domestic and foreign policy is created from a Christian morality-based standpoint, and that is what offends so many people who are not Christian. Furthermore, Christians continually fill the airwaves and other media with their endless fundraising and recruitment of new members ("saving" and "converting"), and that is also offensive to people who are not Christian.

The vast majority of people who do not share Catholic or other Christian beliefs must constantly sit by quietly and absorb - or try to ignore - the unending stream of preaching and endure the everyday skewing of public policy, and be led by a president who mentions his religious values in each speech. A complete separation of church and state clearly do not exist in this country, and for those who do not share the beliefs of the Church, that is offensive.

There is definitely nothing inherently Christian about invading countries who have not attacked us. Nor is there anything Christian about fighting back ("turn the other cheek"). There is nothing Christian about signing the execution order for a retarded person (as G.W. Bush who calls himself a Christian did as governor of Texas).

I find most of Christianity in general to be increasingly less Christian. For those reasons, I could not be happier that people are offended by my artwork. Perhaps those who are offended now feel what it is like to have someone else's ideals paraded in your face as if the country is intolerant of any other views.

I was raised Catholic. I attended 12 years of Catholic schools where I feel I received an excellent, well-rounded education. I love God's creatures and have been vegetarian for 13 years.

I feel like if someone who looks like Jesus looked were to walk up to the window of a modern American Christian's car and ask for food, shelter, help or compassion, they would receive less than what Jesus would hope they would give. Naturally, this is America and everyone is entitled to their own beliefs.

I would urge those who are offended by my art to try to imagine where it may have come from. Look at the country and the world from the other side. And judge not, lest ye be judged.

In the above response, I tried to let people see things from the perspective of non-Christians living in Christian-dominated America. I knew some of my comments would get some goats, but just like the Saint Clinton image itself, I totally underestimated how drastically different than myself a lot of Americans are.

Instead of helping a lot people see my point of view, it seemed to serve only to get them more fired up. It also got them more eager to explain basic things to me that I already knew: i.e. Bill Clinton cheated on his wife, separation of church and state isn't in the Constitution, America was founded by Christians, George W. Bush is a Christian, abortion is unpleasant for everyone involved.

As I told WLKY-TV, I created Saint Clinton to amuse people and to provoke thought. Some people look back on things they did and ask themselves how they could have been so stupid. In the instance of inviting all this criticism and all these verbal attacks, I am so thankful that I acted in a way which others deem to have been so stupid. The unrelenting flood of commentary and email I "asked for" by expressing myself and offering my opinions to those who disagree with my choices has been very eye-opening, to say the least.

I've learned a lot about Americans. I've learned that there is a wide divide between the way Christians and non-Christians see the world. Humor, irony, politics, sanctity, fair game, equal rights, respectfulness and freedom of expression all have totally different meanings to different people, and all combine uniquely in each individual. I have seen that while my opinions of Bill Clinton have sweetened over the years, that is certainly not the case for many others who still have very sour feelings for him. I have seen firsthand, the depressing results of the Bush administration's successful demonization of Muslims and the people of Middle Eastern countries. I've learned that I no longer think Lyndon Johnson was the worst president in modern history. I've learned that angry Christians love using the caps lock key and excessive exclamation points and question marks. I've learned that the more fervent you are in your Christian beliefs, the better chance there is that you never made it past the first round in a spelling bee.

Foreword
ABOUT THE BOOK

This book is comprised primarily of letters and electronic mail messages I've received in response to Saint Clinton and the media coverage of it. These messages have been selected from the hundreds I have received and continue to receive as of this writing. Some of my responses to individual writers appear in this book as well. A few contain a back-and-forth dialogue between myself and the writers. A couple entries are from one writer to another in response to messages that were posted on SaintClinton.com.

The letters I chose to print in this book are the ones that I thought were the funniest, the scariest, the most educated, the most retarded, the kindest, the cruelest, the ones with the most unnecessary punctuation and the biggest lack of punctuation.

The letters are reprinted here in as close to their original form as possible, preserving the writers' misspellings, grammatical errors and personality. I've given each one a title, some of which are quotes from the letters, while others are just titles. Whenever possible, the writer's geographic location is listed. In cases when that information was not available, simply a first name and the domain name from which the message was sent. Some names have been changed to protect privacy.

Offensive and immoral

This is blasphemy!!! How dare anybody put together such trash?? This is wrong and very sad!!!

To take our Sacred heart of Jesus image and post Clinton's face on him?? That is outrageous!!!!

The "I love the abortion" logo on a babies bib and thong is not only disgusting, but is offensive and immoral and very STUPID.

Many Faithful Catholics are very upset and sad over these blasphemies. I hope your happy. :(...

–Kenneth, rgv.rr.com

Your amusement is painful

Regarding your saint clinton image.... your amusement is painful for some, including myself. So you are amused using religion as a joke. Some of us are hurt by your humor............. vs

–Vincent, comcast.net

Think about it

As a Catholic who takes the Sacred Heart of Jesus very seriously, I find it highly offensive that you would place anyone's face of Jesus' in that picture. I find it intolerant, ignorant and insensitive and I urge you to please stop selling your merchandise. You have your opinions and can say Clinton is a saint (which he's not), but please do not defame that picture as is means a lot to Catholics around the world. In addition, I find your baby t-shirts and bibs that say "I love abortion" stupid and disgusting. Why would a baby ever love abortion when abortion would have kept him from being born? Think about it.

—Shirley, yahoo.fr

God is, even though the whole world deny him. Truth stands, even if there be no public support. It is self-sustained - Gandhi

It's crap

Just an opinion on St. Clinton - it's crap. Do something useful in this world instead of getting mileage from a total loser and a total winner. I assume you know the difference, but I could be wrong.

—Dave; Louisville, Kentucky

Your mother should have aborted you

This is the most sickening and revolting thing I've ever seen. It is the basest form of sacrilege – not to mention nauseating… literally!

How sick does someone have to be to condone such trash; but more importantly…how sick and perverted does one have to be to have created such cold and perverted crap????!!!

This is not only offensive to Christians, but to Mothers everywhere!!! Not to mention those who are revolted by Bill Clinton…Democrats and/or Republicans!

You and your group think you are so "in vogue, up-to-the-minute and part of the liberal elite". In fact, you are sad, pitiable and useless. And these trends and fads come and go. When being part of this "liberal elite" passes, you will still be sad, pitiable and useless.

I hope you enjoy your earnings (if any) for this Godless endeavor, because life and your 15 minutes of fame are fleeting and your pathetic little bit of exposure will cost you your soul and an eternity of pain. Your mother should have aborted YOU.

–Pam, glada.com

This message is for "Pam"

This message is for "Pam", who recently wrote, in response to your 'Saint Clinton' image, that your mother should have aborted you.

Pam, that is not a very Christian (or motherly) thing to say. I wonder if Jesus Christ would encourage or embrace your support of abortion. I would imagine not. I wonder if Our Savior would bless your unforgiving, hateful, and judgmental attitude toward this young man.

Pam, surely you know what the Good Book says about judging. "Judge not, lest ye be judged." (Matthew 7:1) I am disturbed that as a woman who identifies herself as aligning with Christianity, you are able to sit in such furious judgment of someone (and his mother) and condemn his soul to "an eternity of pain".

What we now refer to as "The Sacred Heart of Jesus" image, is not a photograph of Christ. It is not a painting or snapshot of Our Lord. It is an artist's rendering (designed in Italy in the 18th century) that Christians have embraced. It has been modified, altered, and updated over the course of hundreds of years. 'Saint Clinton' is also an artist's rendering that you happen not to appreciate.

Pam, I implore you, if you decide to truly follow the teachings of Jesus Christ (rather than using Christianity as an excuse to judge and hate others), you should begin to pray for this young man. He has lost his way, and needs humanity's help to achieve salvation. In the meantime, I will be praying for you, Pam.

Amen,
Pete; Huntsville, Alabama

Please stop

The "saint Clinton" pictures that you have been distributing are quite offensive and insensitive. I ask that you please stop distributing them.

God Bless,
—A.A., aol.com

What's the story?

What's the story on that Saint Clinton stuff? And the "I love abortion" junk? Certainly you realize how disgusting and radically offensive this trash is. What has compelled you to do something so horrid and despicable?

Just wondering... Peace.
—Shaun, yahoo.com

Making the rounds at my office

Dear Scott: I wanted to complement your Saint Clinton page. It is making the rounds at my office. I've just graduated from Law School and taken the Bar Exam. I work for the "old man" now.

I hope you're doing well.
—Brennan; Louisville, Kentucky

I want some

Your Saint Clinton is amazing. I want some buttons. Are you selling them anywhere in Louisville or are you just on the web?

Also, I recently discovered KCM. Fantastic magazine.
—Michael; Louisville, Kentucky

Our forefathers came to this country for religious freedom

Dear Scott Richter,

As a practicing Catholic I find your Saint Clinton merchandise totally offensive. You have taken "artistic license" way too far in your use of a beloved representation of Jesus Christ and defaced it with the image of President Clinton. Hiding behind your First Amendment rights does not give you free reign to cheapen others rights and beliefs for profit. This is something which you probably didn't consider when you came up with this really offensive portrayal of the former president. You have offended many Catholics in this community, as you are probably now aware.

President Clinton did both good things and bad things during his tenure as president and he had human failures as do we all. Only time will tell wether Mr. Clinton is remembered as a great man in is own right, but he is not a Saint nor is he Jesus Christ, just human like the rest of us. I would hope that if you have any conscious, or sense of decency at all, you would reconsider selling this merchandise.

Our forefathers came to this country for religious freedom. I would not mock, nor make fun, of anyone else religion; and I would appreciate it if you would consider not mocking, or making fun, of my religion either.

–Kathy and Jim, juno.com

Monica Jennifer

Dear sir, You seem to have forgotten some other images that could have been added to St. Clinton. Such as, Monica Jennifer, Paula and many others.

–Renee, juno.com

Your ignorance... probably excuses you somewhat

Dear Mr. Richter,

I have no objection to your attempt to portray Bill Clinton as a saint, but your artwork has gone too far in that you have not made him a saint, but a neo-Jesus Christ. That is why the writers in the feedback section are so inflamed. Putting the Sacred Heart symbol on his chest signifies Jesus, not a saint, and indeed is high blasphemy. I'd say "shame on you", but your ignorance of Catholic belief probably excuses you somewhat.

It would have been far more acceptable, and even more tongue-in-cheek, to picture him in a flowing robe with a halo above his head and holding a couple of white lilies which, in religious art, signify purity, a virtue that never got in the way of Clinton's actions.

—Dianne, infionline.net

Ridicule at Christ's expense

I recently viewed the Saint Clinton image and merchandise at your website. Although I'm not Catholic, I am standing with my Catholic brothers and sisters in total disagreement with your co-opting Christ for Clinton and then trying to make money off it. It saddens me that what is sacred to others is fair game for you. Is there nothing motivating in your life except the pursuit of more money? If artistic expression is your driving force, you have failed miserably here. Knowing Christ helps an individual to live by precepts that encourage love and action driven by that love. I will love you by praying for you that you will understand that your actions in creating this image have hurt others by its offensiveness and by your insensitivity. Nothing is accomplished by its creation except ridicule at Christ's expense (which He said would happen*) and your making money off of it. I pray that one day your heart is changed by His.

Jesus is Love
—Frances; Tampa, Florida

*Luke 6:22-26

I wouldn't like George Bush's image as Christ either

Hello: I realize you are an artist, But: I think this is absurd. I would be upset with anyone's image other than Christ himself. IM an artistic person and against censorship. I do believe that sometimes it takes commonsense to make up your mind to do something that would offend people. I wouldn't like George Bush's Image as Christ either. I was raised a catholic, but I am an Episcopalian. Please try to understand why people are offended. IM not some religious nut. I do find some of the 6 Flags over Jesus parishioners a bit much but you have to be tolerant sometimes. I just find this image inappropriate. You may not be religious. I find a lot of artistic people to be very existential minded. I guess if you are a Clinton fan perhaps you find this amusing but he's a serial adulterer. I feel that he was a good Politician but in many way's he was offensive to women. I believe the upbringing he had has a lot to do with the way he conducted his life in office. Oh well""" That's my opinion, everyone has one. Sincerely LA,

—Martinez, aol.com

You'd better study up on what makes a saint

You've got to be kidding! What traits does this man have that qualify him as a "saint?" I think you'd better study up on what makes a saint a saint before you bestow it on someone. The picture is one thing, but dumping your spiritual ignorance on the public through this picture is what really offends me. Be responsible and keep your toxicity to yourself.

—Colleen, insightbb.com

DIALOGUE WITH AN EXCLAMATION AND CAPS LOCK JUNKIE:

An Absolutely digusting idea and not in the least funny!!!!
Clinton is a sleazeball---and a vulgar human being!!!

—unsigned, cs.com

Do you find it disgusting because you are a Christian? If you are a Christian, do you feel it is appropriate to call someone a sleazeball and vulgar human being? Bill Clinton is one of God's children and is just as loved by God as you and I. You and many other people who have sent me messages stating your offense seem to negate your point by behaving in a somewhat less than Christian manner. Judge not, lest ye be judged.
- Scott Ritcher

Personally, I believe he is a gay

Bill Clinton is vulgar and taught my grandchildren from the white house all about oral sex and the vulgar use of cigars!!!

He is, was, always will be a disgrace to the American People and the scriptures state, "have no fellowship with the UNFRUITFUL WORKS OF DARKNESS, BUT RATHER REPROVE THEM" and "THERE IS NONE OTHER NAME GIVEN AMONG MEN WHEREBY YE MUST BE SAVED, JESUS CHRIST" found in Peter.

Also states, "be not DECEIVED, GOD IS NOT MOCKED FOR WHATSOEVER A MAN SOWETH, THAT SHALL HE ALSO REAP" AND ANOTHER SCRIPTURE:

"YE ARE OF YOUR FATHER THE DEVIL AND THE WORKS OF YOUR FATHER YE WILL DO, HE WAS A LIAR

FROM THE BEGINNING AND THE FATHER OF LIES"
BILL CLINTON LIED UNDER OATH AND IS A HATER
OF WOMEN!!!! personally, I believe he is a gay.

—unsigned, cs.com

Because of your insensitivity... I will never vote Democrat

Sir,
Your sacrilege of placing Clinton's head on the Sacred Heart is
beyond all decency. Yes, you have a right to do as you wish
"artistically", but the public also has a right to react. Obviously,
you did not research the figure you have decapitated as that person
was NOT a saint but our Lord.

I will pray for you sir and because of your insensitivity to Christians
and in particular, Catholics, I will never vote Democrat.

You do not have permission to post my name on your website.

—Sally, cox.net
[This may or may not be her real name.]

My Savior wasn't a girlie man (or)
We can sell your body parts to the highest bidders

One of your comments is that some of the Christians writing to
you sounded very un-Christian. Perhaps that's because you believe
all Christians walk around all day saying "Praise the Lord," while
patting children on the head. I don't know about you, but my
Savior wasn't a girlie man :) He IS God. Your art is pathetic--a
sign of the times. Tell you what . . . you check out our novel at

www.thecalltoprayer.net as I've checked out your miserable T-Shirt. Then we'll compare notes. And, for the record, why would you make a baby bib that says "I love abortion." Maybe we should stuff you in a balloon filled with warm solution and let you rest there for awhile until you're really secure and comfortable. Then, when you least suspect it, we'll grab you by one leg, pull it into the neck of the balloon, then grab the other leg and do the same until only your head is stuck in the balloon, the rest of you in the neck. We'll then trace a finger up your spine until we find the base of your skull and stab with a sharp object, widen the hole, and suck our your brains. How does that sound? When we're done and your dead, we can sell your body parts to the highest bidders, most of whom donate their profits to the liberals.

I'm going to something rather radical for you. I'm going to pray for you and put you on thousands of prayer lists. The Hound of Heaven will be after you, sir, until you bow a knee before Him in repentance. I can only hope the slob Bill Clinton has the smarts (his brain is too small and too low on his body) to rebuke what you've done.

I feel sorry for you.

In His Grip,
—Jill; Hixson, Tennessee

The only thing funnier than the picture...

Re: St. Clinton - I thought it was a riot. The only thing funnier than the picture itself were the comments against them. Lighten up people!

—Nancy, hotmail.com

COST OF WAR IN IRAQ
APPROVED BY CONGRESS APRIL 4 2003 & NOV 4 2003
VS.
2004 Annual Budgets of Selected Government Departments

ONE BLOCK ■ REPRESENTS ONE BILLION DOLLARS

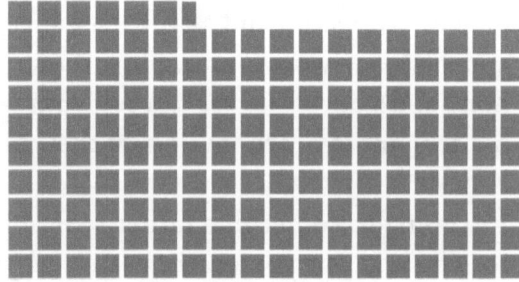

Environmental Protection Agency
$7.6 billion

Department of Energy
$23.4 billion

Department of Education
$53.1 billion

War in Iraq
$167.5 billion

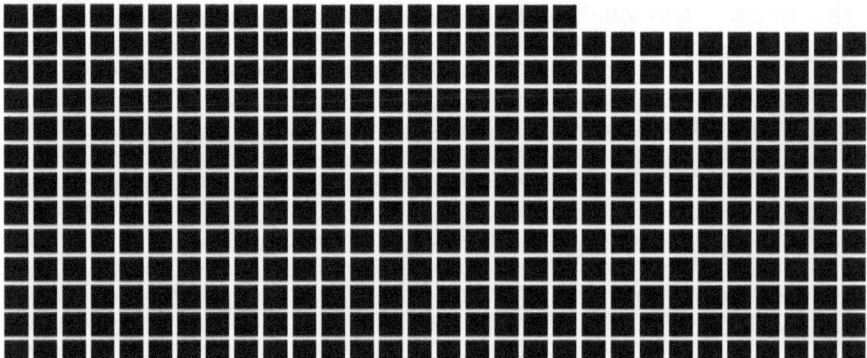

Department of Defense (regular annual budget not including Iraq)
$380 billion

FIG.2: The cost of the war and occupation of Iraq as of early 2004, when combined with the Dept of Defense's 2004 annual budget, is nearly 7 times more than the COMBINED 2004 budgets of the Dept of Education, Dept of Energy and the Envirnomental Protection Agency.

The effort in Iraq breaks down to a cost of approximately $600 per American. Due to Bush's tax cuts, the sluggish economy and the fact that wars are unpredictable and therefore not entirely included in the annual budget, most of the costs for US action in Iraq and Afghanistan are being financed by loans. These loans are added to the National Debt, to be paid off after Bush leaves office.

SOURCE: WHITE HOUSE OFFICE OF MANAGEMENT & BUDGET.
TEXT EXCERPTED FROM NEWSNSHIT.COM CURRENT EVENTS HOMEPAGE.

I've got news for you

I've got news for you, as I often do for the intellectually deplete.........
Bill Clinton had ABSOLUTELY NOTHING to do with the
booming 90's economy, and I challenge you to give us one thing
he did to even phase it! He simply enjoyed the credit for the
results of Reagan's work.

Oh by the way, there are two sets of saints in history; the ones
who were pretty good, and the ones who were extremely corrupt.
I think we know which one Bill belongs in.

—Greg; Raleigh, North Carolina

Simple, meaningless

I consider this art to be similar in approach to Serrano's piss
Christ, the dung-flung Madona and the dress-up peel and stick
Jesus. Simple, meaningless, and a reflection of the artist mind,
heart and perspective. I think a more obviously sarcastic, creative
and appropriate image for Clinton would have been Christ's
apostle, who three times denied the truth, Saint Peter.

—Mike, sbcglobal.net

"Superimposting"

I am writing to voice my outrage at the irreverent, sacrilegious
picture you have depicted of Bill Clinton as the "Sacred Heart."
The representation of Jesus Christ as the Sacred Heart has
been revered and venerated for centuries by Catholics all over the
world. By superimposting Bill Clinton's head over the face of

Christ, you have mocked the beautiful image and representation of Christ.

I am asking that you take down this blasphemous picture from your website and stop any further commercialization of this sacrilegious image.

—Ann, yahoo.com

Signing the execution form for a retarded person

Ah...sweet irony. You challenge President George W. Bush's Christian bona fides by accusing him of signing the execution form for a retarded person. Maybe you're referring to Ricky Ray Rector. He was executed after the governor left the campaign trail to make sure the execution took place. Funny thing is the governor was from Arkansas and his name was BILL CLINTON and the execution took place in January 1992, while he was running for president. He wanted to show how tough he was. Rick Ray Rector was so retarded that he saved his dessert from his last meal so he could eat it the next day. Just like most liberals, you are ill informed and you look silly when you try to make political points. Stick to the stupid art and save us the commentary.

—Ken, insightbb.com

Ken, Thanks for the information. I stand corrected and will leave the execution of mentally handicapped individuals out of my future criticisms of Bush. - Scott

The State has replaced God in the religion of the Left

I find your Saint Clinton graven image to be an utterly appropriate one. It slams home the idea that the State has replaced God in the religion of the Left. The use of the apostate Bill Clinton as the messiah of this group is utterly appropriate. Also fitting would be the use of his wife Hillary in the role of madonna.

—Tom, us.thales-bm.com

Are you the anti-Christ? Please advise.

Dear Sir:
Your St. Clinton is disgraceful and a sacrilege. Exodus 20- "I am the Lord, your God. You shall not false gods besides me." You have disgraced the picture of the Sacred Heart of Jesus. When you meet God at the hour of your death, you will burn in hell if you do not repent. Are you the anti-Christ? Please advise. It is not your decision, sir, who decides who saints are. That belongs to the Holy Father. I urge you for your own good to stop this nonsense to save your soul and in the intersts of common decency.

Respectfully,
—Jack, yahoo.com

Semantics: "retarded" vs. "mentally handicapped"

Hey artist. Read your note about your art and so called Christian reaction to it. Ya'll have a good time with all that, but what struck me was the mentioning of Mr. Bush executing a retarded man in Texas. Don't you remember Mr. Clinton going back to Arkansas to execute a mentally handicapped person when he was running for the top job in 1992?? Oh, maybe it's the difference in semantics.

—Lesley, woh.rr.com

The ACLU is the biggest threat to all our freedoms (or) Evolutionists believe that the colored races are less evolved

Scott Ritcher,
First of all I would like to say that you have some sever honesty in your written speech seen on "Worldnet Daily". I am a Christian and I'm also appalled at the way some Christians act and react to society. The truth is, it could be that many of them are not Christians at all or just simply acting on the flesh for which we all are made of.

Secondly I would like to say that your view of the Separation of Church and State is backwards. This was never meant to keep the church out of politics or the state but to keep the state/politics out of the church. This is actually the exact opposite of ho the statement is viewed and used. Think about it! America was founded on freedoms, that which we receive from God, it from men nor women nor any government. The problem lies in the fact that if we all realized that our value and worth came from God himself, we wouldn't need to have women's rights, civil rights, or gay rights. We already have them from above. They need not be laid in stone again or written in blood in the court rooms or law offices. They can all be found in the Bible, God's Holy Word. That is where we have lost focus. Whether you believe in it or not is beside the point, you would still have those inalienable God given rights, if they are being governed and enforced by those who know them and have the correct relationship with God.

As far as Christians on the airwaves and TV., you as an American have the right to turn them off. That would be a true use of your rights. The sad thing is that Christians get upset because we are continually forced to accept the beliefs and values of others, our freedom taken away, when we do not get the same treatment. I cannot tell you how many times the lifestyles, or beliefs of other groups are shown in full capacity on TV., advertising or written about in society to the extreme. If we choose not to agree, we are called haters and a black label id giving to us. Why does this never work in the opposite direction? I already know the true answer, I'm being rhetorical.

The ACLU is the biggest threat to all of our freedoms I believe. Why, because we are being forced to give in, or not to have an opinion on our own moral standards or beliefs. We are being forced to accept the beliefs or life choices of others. That is not freedom, it is the very absence of it. The civil liberties they fight for is eroding the very heart of the basics of our country and what it stands for. No matter what color, race or lifestyle you choose, you have the same rights! Why can we simply not leave it at that? Why are there special rights for these groups? Are they not American citizens? If a black man is killed or a gay man is robbed does there citizenship change? If the law breaker is caught, then prosecute them as the law ordains. I simply do not understand the very nature of their fight. Do you require special attention because you were victimized? Should a black man killed get more or less attention than a gay man killed? Are they both not counted as a loss?

Let me give you an everyday example to better understand or make more clear my point. I can and will truly say that I a problem with the gay life style. I do not agree with it. That does not mean I hate or will not associate with those who choose this lifestyle. That is simply my opinion and I'm entitled to it. It's an American right given to me! Before I receive some hate mail, end up in court or I'm called a name or two, let me explain. That is simply my opinion and belief. I have that right, just as you or anyone else does to support or live that life style. As a Christian, I'm also called to love that person with that lifestyle and/or that opinion. Again, because of my Christian beliefs, I am to love and accept this person with this lifestyle, but I do not have to agree with it. Do we not all have friends or co-workers that we get along with but do not always agree with the choices they make? Is this any different than the previous example? Would it not be better to have this type of lifestyle and to have a Christian friend or leader who is called to love and accept your choice, but just not support it? Unfortunately this type of love-the-person-hate-the-sin type of viewpoint is many times not undertaken by Christians or those claiming to be Christians.

Lets face it, life is not easy. When growing up, if you're overweight, if you're too skinny, if you have bad acne, or if you don't wear the new stylish clothes you are picked on or looked down upon. That's life! I'm not saying it's fair, but what I am saying is that there does not need to be a law stating that you have every right to have acne, be poor, be skinny or to be fat. Is that not ludicrous? We already have laws or people in authority to deal with these situations and to teach people to be tolerant of others because we are all different. Unfortunately, we cannot use corporal punishment any longer to go along with the speeches made by teachers or administrative faculty. We are forced to put the offender out in the hall or away from the other students (which isolates them and may even strengthen their misunderstanding or unacceptability) as punishment. This many times creates a greater gap in understanding or tolerance by isolating them to form their own little group or viewpoint rather than facing the responsibility and dealing with it in the present. The way our society is going, you will be breaking a law to even have an opinion. I almost wrote, "You will be breaking the law by calling someone names or even having the thought of calling them a name because they are different". Believe it or not that those very laws are already written in a book. Again the Bible. Jesus taught it from the Sermon on the Mount. Yes, we will even be judged by our very thoughts and it is only God who knows them and will judge us righteously because of them. Wow, laws and decrees which judge by our very thoughts and schemes. I bet many of you weren't even aware that they existed. Once again, the view of Christianity (God is the only righteous and true judge) is so far from any human viewpoint of law making or forethought of fairness in judgment created by man. Yes, the Bible was written by man, but it was inspired by the Spirit of God to be written. I guess it makes more sense when you realize why many, if not most of our forefathers who wrote the Constitution, The Bill of Rights and the Declaration of Independence were Christian and practiced their Christian beliefs in their life and most importantly in their jobs/responsibilities to their country.

Again, if we could all embrace the idea that we are all made equal, all with God given rights and abilities, than we would have no problem. When we begin to accept the fact that we were created by an all knowing, all powerful, all loving God rather than the idea (yes an idea, not proving fact) that we evolved from an apelike man we would begin to embrace the fact that we all have God given value and worth. We need not receive it from any human source, although God does command us to have a mutual respect of each other and to encourage and embrace one another. It's all about relationships, the most important being one with God then others. For with out God, how do we know how to have the proper view of love and relationship. Do you know that a book which is still used in our public schools today (Teaching About Evolution) which teaches evolution, states that since we evolved from ancient apelike men we are all not at the same steps in evolution. Evolutionists believe that the colored races are less evolved and are less advanced rationally or cognitively? Is that not hate crime or racial in intent? Why is that not being dealt with? I'll tell you why. Because the only other alternative which has as much proven fact or is the next best and equally possible hypothesis is the creation example/belief laid out in the Bible! That's why!

To get to the matter of your Clinton imagery, I do not agree with it and I believe it is sacrilegious! In the truth of the matter, I feel that you have taken an image meant to honor God and have defaced it. But, it is only an image! The second biggest problem is that we as a society do things like this and say it's just for humor. If we really had the proper view of an all holy and righteous God, we would not ever use God in a fashion to be made humorous. Yes, you have the rights as an American to make the image. I just do not agree with it. Will I push for a law banning you to not be able to ever make an image like it again? Certainly not, although as far as the ACLU seems to be concerned, I should be able to have their support in having the image banned and never able to be fashioned again, because it misrepresents/offends my personal beliefs and goes against my freedom of religion. Yes, again I'm being sarcastic, but here is a grain of truth to the statement. I believe that there is already a law you have broken, and it is found in the ten commandments (#3). This is a sin that you will have to deal with and it's no laughing matter. I'm just letting you know about it and asking you to not to use it for our own sake.

If you want my honest opinion about your Clinton imagery, it is a marketing scheme by which you are being used to make money off of those you will make this a war on differences of opinion (Republicans vs. Democrats). If you do make money from it, how about using it in a way which gives praise to God, not offends Him!

–Shaun, diosynth-rtp.com

Sainthood is only a one-step promotion from the current near universal regard for Pres. Clinton

I saw the article in WorldNetDaily. As a Christian, but not a Catholic, I feel that sainthood is only a one-step promotion from the current near universal regard for Pres. Clinton.

I would vote the three following items on the WorldNetDaily poll:
- Making Clinton look godly is impossible, so I find this humorous.
- It's just a joke, too much is being made of this.
- It's a misguided portrait of the Democrats' idealistic delusional self-image.

—Mark; Olney, Maryland

I don't use the word "blasphamy" lightly

Though there are many things which people have done to ridcule and make fun of 'all' religions and I find your picture depicting of the Sacred Heart of Jesus with the head of Bill Clinton very disheartening. A question you should ask yourself, is; Am I comparing Jesus to Bill Clinton or am I comparing Bill Clinton to Jesus or what is my purpose; to just be funny? No matter which it is, it is wrong and I don't think any 'real' Christian or 'non' Christian would agree with or find any humor in it as well. Contrary to what others may have said, I do not condemn you. Through my Catholic faith I have learned that Jesus judges us but, we condemn ourselves. You may want to re-think your actions of both your 'I love abortion baby bibs' or other questionable articles you have may have produced including the blasphamy of using Bill Clinton's head on a Sacred Heart of Jesus picture. I do not use the word "blasphamy" lightly. This is a very serious accusation. I think if Bill Clinton were to see his face being used in this manner he would disagree with it too.

Best Wishes.
—Tom, sbcglobal.net

Bush is not the bad guy (or)
The invasion of Iraq "had to happen to fulfill Bible prophecy"

Mr. Ritcher,

I would like to bring a little light to the table on your painting
and your obvious attempts to be funny and why you are wrong
and why people are mad. There are plenty of things in this world
to make fun of but when you bring God or Jesus in the picture
you cross lines morally and spiritually. Claiming that "Christians"
are not acting like "Christians" well there are two kinds of anger,
there is an anger that is sinful in nature and there a righteous
anger when defending the works of Jesus and making any kind of
play against the savior of the world, the original painting which
portrays Jesus has no business being altered in that manner. Artist
call it "art" because you bring your twisted thoughts and put
them to canvas and modify a sacred holy picture of Christ, an
compare the picture with a pathological liar, adulterer, and
murderer (yes wake up read the reports Clinton not doing anything
in 1999 brought on the terror attacks against this country!! Bush
is not the bad guy he is the one dealing with the incompetence
handed to him from the lacking of the previous administration)
You quote a few bible verses like you think you know what you
are talking about. You make comments like "turn the other cheek"
and a "Christian country" invades a country who didn't attack
us, first off we did not invade Iraq to take over Iraq we invaded
Saddam and his military, and we are trying to rebuild the country
and let the people govern themselves, but since your such the
bible scholar you also know it had to happen to fulfill bible
prophecy, but I am sure you already knew that... You use the
scripture judging, do you have any idea what that scripture means?
by your standards of response I would say no. You make comments
about the Christian believers who peddle their beliefs in this

country and shove it down everyone's throat, well bible scholar you obviously must have not read the great commission written by our Lord in the book of Matthew 16:15, your bible says that Christians are salt and light, do you know what that means? maybe you should make an attempt to really find out! I am not even going to say anything about your "I love abortion bibs" you already have enough to answer to God about but the picture blasphemes the Lord Jesus and I truly hope your eyes are opened in this matter. For the sake of your soul, it is not to late to rescind this material and ask God for forgiveness.

–Brandon; Indiana

You are like the computer genius who creates viruses

You are like the computer genius who creates viruses instead of helpful programs. WHY? You are a good artist—why don't you use your talent for good?

Hopefully Bill Clinton will be given the grace to conform his life to your rendition of him. Personally, I feel that Jesus would be insulted (if such a thing were possible, which I doubt).

I read that you are a former Catholic who feels you were given a good education. Evidently you were not given the correct education about your faith (most of us weren't). I will keep you in my prayers because you have a long, bumpy road ahead of you. I've been down that road myself and will ask God to enlighten and to bless you with the truth!

–Beth, mindspring.com

Satan hated the Lord's love for man

Scott,

I recently read an article on your works here: http://www.worldnetdaily.com/news/article.asp?ARTICLE_ID=40523

I frequent worldnetdaily because many of its articles point out what I consider to be today's issues and worthy of prayer. I pray the Spirit of Truth would do a great work on His canvas which is you, Scott Ritcher.

In Genesis 1 we read, "So God created man in his own image, in the image of God he created him." Now you are an artist, I want you to realize the beautiful picture God is recording for us here as "the Lord God formed the man from the dust of the ground and breathed into his nostrils the breath of life" (Genesis 2:7). And I want you to realize the exalted position to which God assigned both you and me when God said, "fill the earth and subdue it. Rule over ...{all things}" (Genesis 1:28). Lovingly, God placed the man in His garden with trees that were "pleasing to the eye and good for food" (Genesis 2:8).

And so man lacked nothing. He was built to perfection; he was placed over all things; he was given a pleasing home. One thing, however, God required: that man should not eat of the tree of knowledge of good and evil, Genesis 2.

Now the deceiver, that is Satan, challenged the woman to eat of the tree of the knowledge of good and evil because Satan hated the Lord's love for man. Believing that the fruit of the forbidden tree was desirable, the woman and the man destroyed their relationship with God by consuming the fruit. As the man and woman were hiding in the garden in their newly found nakedness they sought out a few leaves by which to insufficiently cover themselves, Genesis 3:7. And while they were in their sin God sought them and called for them, Gen 3:8. In verse 15 of chapter 3 God declares war on the devil, a war to which Christians have already won through Christ Jesus. And the Lord looked lovingly upon the man and woman and in verse 21 He made garments of skin to replace the leaves which were covering them. In love the Lord removed the man and woman from the garden so that they would not live forever in their sin.

Scott, you have read these passages before. Do you see the war which is going on for your very soul? But "God made him {Jesus Christ} who had no sin to be sin for us" (2 Corinthians 5:21). And His Son {Jesus Christ}, purifies us from all sin" (1 John 1:7). In fact the Lord cursed Himself for our salvation!!!!! It is written in Galatians 3:13, "Cursed is everyone who is hung on a tree." And this is in accordance to Deuteronomy 21:22,23. Do you see the pain Jesus endured as He cried out, "My God, my God, why have you forsaken me?" (Matthew 27:45).

Because God did not leave us to be cursed, but loved each of us so much as to sacrifice His only Son and curse Him in our steed; Christian throughout the world and throughout time hold to glorifying God. As in Revelations 5:12 we declare, "Worthy is the Lamb, who was slain, to receive power and wealth and wisdom and strength and honor and glory and praise!"

By defacing the Lord as you have in your work, St. Clinton, you have saddened any Christian who holds to what I have written above. When the Lord has given His all for you, Scott, do not defame His name. While I pray the deceiver would loose his grip on the world, today I pray for you Scott Ritcher. May the Lord reveal Himself to you and work a great work on the canvas of your soul.

In Christ whose words are Truth,
–Greg, earthlink.com

You make a mockery of... every human who has ever been... unjustly tortured, beaten, mocked or humiliated

Having been raised a Roman Catholic, you probably know the story of Christ's passion.

I just wanted to share with you a brief thought:

"And plaiting a crown of thorns, they put it upon His head...And they mocked Him, saying Hail, King of the Jews"

Whether you believe that the man who beaten, scorned and mocked one Friday was anything more than a man, what good can come from mocking a man in those circumstances? Any man. There is an inherent dignity in every human individual, solely by virtue of their humanity. No person can give us that. No one can take it away.

I think the kind of mockery you portray here tries to take peoples' individual human dignity away. You make a mockery of many people's idea of a beloved image of their God; you make a cruel mockery of Mr Clinton; you make a mockery of that mysterious man who was crucified 2000 years ago, and of every human who has ever been - or is being right now, today - unjustly tortured, beaten, mocked and humiliated. The world surely does not need more of this, regardless of your intent.

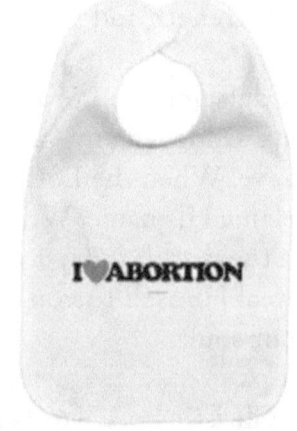

Peace
—Sandy, msn.com

FIG. 3:
"I LOVE ABORTION" BABY BIB
(DISCONTINUED)

DIALOGUE WITH A GUY NAMED DOUG:

These assholes are absolutely crazy. This pinhead is no more a Saint then he is trustworthy. Goes to show what some good ole backwoods ingenuity can really produce. It must really disappoint you hillbilly's knowing that Clinton doesn't wear a mullet, or you'd have the ultimate portrait. "Kentucky: Five Million People; Fifteen Last Names"

—Doug, verizon.net

Doug,
Based on the words spelled incorrectly in your missive, I feel you shouldn't be the one calling other assholes hillbillies. Maybe you should have your mom look over your letters in the future before you hit the "send" button.
- Scott.

I'm sure it's hard for you to keep going back to the dictionary to check your spelling Scott. (Notice the capital "S" here). I'm sure somewhere in the backwoods you can find a computer with spell check and even grammar check if you want! It's got to be hard for you to determine when something is written intentionally, ("ole") Scott. Maybe you should take some of you own advice. Have your mom look your letters over before you push the "send" button. Or maybe you can have your sister do the same, after all in Kentucky they both may be the same person.

—Doug, verizon.net

Hey Doug,
I was speaking of the words "then" which should be "than" and "hillbilly's" which should be "hillbillies." I understood that "ole" was intentional, and apparently you thought that was the only unusual spelling in your letter. I'm glad we had this little talk. You can thank me in heaven.
Love, Scott.

DOUG (continued):

Thanks for pointing that out. We don't have many opportunities (?) to use the word Hillbilly much out here.

Be careful Scott showing up to the pearly gates with that Saint Clinton picture in your hands. The last time I checked there was no Saint Clinton. That might be a big mistake. So I'd better thank you now.

Thanks
–Doug, verizon.net

Anyone who is angry, doesn't get my sympathy; they should just turn it off

Scott:

I read an article concerning your "Saint Clinton" artwork and humor. It was posted on world Net Daily. I found a few things interesting and wanted to share my opinion:

1. You indicate that "Christians continually fill the airwaves and other media with their endless fundraising and recruitment of new members ("saving" and "converting"), and that is also offensive to people who are not Christian."

While this is true, the fact remains that anyone who is offended by the Christians and their Media messages may tune out the radio/tv station and/or not read and purchase the written media. Christians, just like non-christians, use the media to reach a broad audience. Fortunately, in this country, no one can force anyone to listen to it or read it--so anyone who is angry, doesn't get my sympathy; they should just turn it off.

2. "So much of American domestic and foreign policy is created from a Christian morality-based standpoint, and that is what offends so many people who are not Christian."

Unfortunately, this country was founded by Christians on Christian precepts; this includes the freedom of Religion--that is why non-Christians, Jews, Hindus, Muslims, Buddists, and every other religious group, including those who practice the Black Arts, are free to worship as they wish. In most countries where the government controls the religion, no other worship is tolerated. We should be thankful that the Christian principles that our founding fathers stood for allow everyone freedom in this country.

3. "The vast majority of people who do not share Catholic or other Christian beliefs must constantly sit by quietly and absorb – or try to ignore – the unending stream of preaching and endure the everyday skewing of public policy, and be led by a president who mentions his religious values in each speech."

Again, in as much as we are a CHRISTIAN nation (read your money--IN GOD WE TRUST), we should be guided by Christian principles. For those who don't like the President or his values, they should vote to change things. The president isn't all powerful; people give him too much credit. But, this president is a CHRISTIAN-- he admits it and he exercises his right to freedom of religion. For those who are not US citizens who do not like the president, they are free to return to their country of birth. As a matter of fact, no one--US Citizen or otherwise--is forced to remain here. If you don't like our Public Policy, why don't you go to China and see if theirs is a bit more to your liking? It's not based on Christian beliefs, so you won't have to have the Christian Nuts skewing policy; you'll be free to worship as the Government dictates.

4. "A complete separation of church and state clearly do not exist in this country, and for those who do not share the beliefs of the Church, that is offensive."

I am very disappointed in your Catholic Education. If you had a good education, as you claim, you would realize that there is NOTHING in the Constitution guaranteeing "Separation of Church and State". This is something Madeline Murray O'Hare and her Liberal Cronies created and have been propagating for the past 40 years.

The BILL OF RIGHTS, First Amendment to the CONSTITUTION reads: "Congress shall make no law respecting an establishment of religion, or prohibiting the free exercise thereof; or abridging the freedom of speech, or of the press; or the right of the people peaceably to assemble, and to petition the Government for a redress of grievances."

Whereas, it specifically states Congress shall make no law respecting the establishment of a religion; it doesn't indicate that Congress cannot act on Christian principles; nor does it say, the President cannot be a Christian and allow his religion to guide his duties. None of your arguments are found here--but what it does say, is that the Government of the US cannot tell you--SCOTT RITCHER--how to worship.

Something that amazes me about you anti-Christians is that in your "Separation of Church and State" argument, you ignore the clause that states "...or prohibiting the free exercise thereof." See, the Bill of Rights doesn't disallow Santa on the Court House Lawn; nor does it forbid the Ten Commandments from display in public buildings. None of these things establish a religion, but the "separation of Church and State" argument tries to forbid anyone from freely exercising their (Christian) religion in public.

5. One thing the First Amendment also guarantees is your freedom of Speech--which the horrendous images you sell as "art" fall under. In this country, you have the right to portray Bill Clinton as a Saint. Although it is disgusting, and morally offensive to me and other Christians, we can protest by not buying it. It would be totally contrary to our Government to forbid you to market it--and I'm sure Bill Clinton loves the image you portray of him.

You say you were raised Catholic. So was I. I remain Catholic to this day, and I wouldn't trade my faith for anything. However, in spite of the poor taste of your art--the biggest offense I find is that you have denigrated Jesus. Whether you believe it or not, many of us believe that Jesus sacrificed HIMSELF for all of us; and to equate Jesus, who is LOVE and LOVE ONLY, with Bill Clinton, who is NOT LOVE, is offensive. I may not like Bill Clinton's actions. I definitely don't like his politics, but I am not able to judge him; his future is between him and Jesus. I can guess, however, that if he were asked to sacrifice his life for the people of the US, Clinton wouldn't do it. Heck, I doubt he's sacrifice his life for Hillary. But Jesus DID sacrifice HIS LIFE for the People of the US. And for the People everywhere else in the world--including the World's Terrorists; including Saddam Hussein; including Bin Ladin; and even including Scott Ritcher. Jesus is LOVE. By superimposing Bill Clinton's face over the Sacred Image of Jesus, you have offended many; no human is equal to Jesus--because I don't think there's a person on this earth who would do for others what Jesus did for us.

Although what I am saying may not agree with your belief; it isn't foreign to anyone raised in a Catholic School. I'm not trying to "shove" my religion on you, but rather explain why your "art" is so offensive to so many.

You have the freedom to create anything; and people have the freedom to buy it, wear it, display it. That's due to the CHRIST-IAN NATURE of our country; in another country, you may have been stoned for blasphemy; other countries aren't nearly as tolerant. Tell me why you chose to depict Clinton as Christ? Why not as St Lucifer? Would that have offended too many non-Christians? As a Christian, it still would have offended me--as I don't enjoy anything that mocks people or my religion. And good or bad, such portrayals mock my religious beliefs.

6. Finally, I must agree with your assessment, "I find most of Christianity in general to be increasingly less Christian." This is true of PEOPLE. Christianity--the CHURCH--as a foundation hasn't changed; but the people who call themselves 'christian' have. Too many people think that it's a one-shot deal--Announce to the World that You are Christian and IT'S DONE! Not true, Christians must live their beliefs (as should all religious people); Think back to your Catholic School Days--Just because we want to be "good Catholics" doesn't make us so. The road to Hell is paved with Good Intentions. The road to Heaven is paved with the love (Blood) of Christ; but just because we say we love HIM, doesn't make it so.

I sense you have left the Church--which is also your right--but regardless of your belief on Earth; once you die, one of two things will happen:

1. Nothing. You'll die, and be gone because your earthly assertions were true. There is no Christian Truth, no Heaven, no Hell. You were right and those of us who pursued a greater good wasted our time.

2. You'll find out you were wrong. You will find out that Jesus is VERY REAL. More importantly, you'll find out that GOD THE FATHER is VERY REAL, and HE is very offended by anyone

who denigrates HIS SON. Once you find out that Jesus is REAL, and GOD is REAL, it follows that you'll find out SATAN is REAL.

Seems to me that it's too late once we die to find out that everything we denied is REAL, and all that we embraced is false. See, I'd rather live my life for Jesus and find out when I die that I was "wrong" than live my life against Jesus and find out when I die that I was "WRONG". It's my choice.

I recommend a video. You may or may not believe in Jesus. You may or may not believe in Heaven and/or Hell; but this video is powerful. It's Called "Her Life After Death" and it's about a woman who "died", met Jesus, and was returned to Life. Hearing her description of seeing someone CHOSE HELL upon their death has haunted me for months.

I wish you peace. You are full of anger and hatred at Christians and you're taking it out on the faith into which you were born and raised. People make mistakes; but Jesus didn't. The offense is that you equate Bill Clinton to the most perfect Son of God.

Sincerely,
—Tress, yahoo.com

Dear Tress,

Thanks for writing and for the time, consideration and thought you put into your message. I can tell that you are a person with strong conviction in your beliefs.

I feel that many of the points you made in response to my commentary served only to illustrate my point of view in greater detail.

In point #1, you say to non-Christians who don't like the constant stream of Christian broadcasting, "anyone who is angry, doesn't get my sympathy; they should just turn it off." I almost collapsed in disbelief when I read that statement! I could have said the exact same thing in response to my critics. The difference is even in my favor: the images I created that some have found offensive are posted on a web site which requires the viewer to deliberately navigate to it. If you don't like my art, don't type the URL of my site into your browser, or don't click on a link someone sends you if you think you'll find it offensive. I couldn't have said it any better than you did, "anyone who is angry, doesn't get my sympathy; they should just turn it off."

For point #2, I find it really hard to believe that freedom of religion is a Christian precept, and I base that purely on the fact that one of the main principles of Christianity is the idea of spreading the Word and bringing new believers into the flock. That's like saying, "You can believe whatever you want, but if you don't believe in Jesus, we're still going to try to change your mind." That doesn't sound like freedom of religion to me. My conclusion is, then, that freedom of religion is a common sense concept, and it just so happens that the people who instituted the idea in America were Christians. Their Christian values may have influenced their concept of government insofar as they respected others and wished to be treated the same, but many religions share that value. I may just be splitting semantic hairs here, but I would say that freedom of religion is as common sense a value as any other freedom or right.

Point #3, I don't even know where to begin with this one. You start off by stating that the United States is a Christian nation as if it is a fact, and then base the rest of your argument on that. In point #2 you state that US citizens have freedom of religion, then you claim in capital letters that we are a Christian nation. If one is true the other cannot be.

The motto "In God We Trust" was an early 20th Century addition to our currency, and you'll notice that it is always in all caps, so as not to be specific to the capitalized Christian "God." Many religions refer to their god as "God" – so the use of the English word "god" is not necessarily an invocation of Christianity. Furthermore, the fact that our currency does say "In God We Trust" makes some of my other points more emphatic; especially my opposition to the influence of Christian-based morality in US policy, because the movement to add that slogan to our money was spearheaded by Christians who felt we needed to recognize a higher power and moral guide as the US went into war.

You finish up your third point with the most immature, redneck offense that Americans give each other, "If you don't like (it), why don't you go to China...?" and "no one is forced to remain here." Give me a break. What the people who throw these lines around don't realize is that the reason people are upset and calling for change is because they think we as a nation could do better. It's not that we hate America or we think it's better everywhere else. It's that we are Americans and we want our country to be the best it can be for everyone's benefit. That's why people like me are raising a stink. If people didn't show any opposition, women wouldn't have the right to vote, child labor laws wouldn't be in place, abortions would be performed by untrained outlaws, and the Christians would get away with more swaying of the national agenda than they already do.

Sure, George W. Bush is a Christian man, but the more he invokes his religion, the more dedicated people who hate America will become in fighting their holy wars against us, for which American citizens and personnel ultimately become the innocent victims. Naturally, this is not the ONLY reason politicians' religious beliefs should stay out of speeches and comments. Another good reason is that it alienates Americans who do not believe the same things. Imagine how you'd feel if you wanted to be a proud American, but the president was an atheist and constantly made reference to there being no God. You would be very disillusioned and would not want to support him, regardless of how sensible his policies were. I feel this is one of the reasons the country is so divided right now. I think we'd be able to find very few American Jews or Muslims who feel good about Bush, and aside from his arrogant and disrespectful foreign policies, his insistence on reminding us of his faith in Christ is a big reason.

The separation of church and state comes into play in point #4. I know that this separation is not outlined in the Constitution. I never said it was. And believe me, I definitely know what the First Amendment is all about. I think what we have here is a part of the ongoing disagreement in this country over the letter of the law vs. the spirit of the law.

Your interpretation of the First Amendment is VERY different than mine. To you, the phrase, "Congress shall make no law respecting an establishment of religion, or prohibiting the free exercise thereof," means that the Ten Commandments, Christmas decorations and other items of religious origins can be displayed on public property. To me, that phrase of the First Amendment means just the OPPOSITE, and the sticking point comes down to the fact that they used the wording "make no law" rather than "take no action." I feel that if the government is not allowed to make laws regarding any particular religion, they should definitely not be allowed to do anything else that could be seen as an act of endorsement or belittlement of any religion.

I agree that the religious beliefs of all elected and appointed officials influence their policies to some degree. That is impossible to prevent or hide. I have no problem with that, so long as it's done in a way that's respectful of the beliefs of others, American or not. I feel that President Bush expresses his beliefs in a divisive and flagrant way. I believe that all policy should be made from the standpoints of ethics, equal rights and equal protection, rather than from the standpoint of morality. I often get the impression that many Christians believe ethics and morals are synonymous words. They certainly are not.

In point #5 the First Amendment is discussed as it pertains to protecting my right to sell imagery which others find to be offensive. People definitely do have a wide range of opinions concerning what I'm doing. I have received several notes from conservative Christians and Catholics who have told me that they think the "Saint Clinton" picture and the "I Love Abortion" items are hilarious, and have purchased them.

Also here, you speculate on what President Clinton's preferences are and what he might do if faced with the choice of his life or his wife's. This is almost as silly as your love-it-or-leave-it comments. So many people have felt the need to explain to me that Bill Clinton is not equal to Jesus and to remind me of Clinton's transgressions. I know, okay? I knew before I made the piece. At no time did I ever feel like I was equating these two men. I also do not feel like I denigrated Jesus. I made a picture of someone else DRESSED like an 18th Century Italian artist's conceptualization of a white man who is representative of Jesus. I think we all know that Jesus, as a fisherman or son of a carpenter in Jerusalem in the 1st Century wasn't wealthy enough to wear gold-lined, brightly colored garments. And we all know he wasn't white. All this outrage over a picture seems to me to be the praising of a false idol - a picture. Even without President Clinton's features attributed to it, the work on which the image is based is outrageously inaccurate that I find most of the arguments moot.

Your letter finishes by making one of two false assumptions made by dozens of those who have written me. It seems you assume I don't believe in God. I do. I am a member of a non-Christian religion that shares much of the same value set, and I believe in living my life in accordance with many of Jesus' teachings, especially respect for others. I have great respect for most of the people who have expressed their views to me about "Saint Clinton," but I just don't agree with what many of them say.

While you didn't accuse me of the second false assumption, many people have assumed that the person who would make such a picture is a Democrat. That I'm not. I have never been a Democrat or a Republican, and until George W. Bush's presidency, I have always felt that both parties were equally abhorrent and corrupt. Bush's administration has done such an effective job of dividing our nation, destroying our respect in the world, squandering children's money, killing innocent people in countries that never attacked ours, and getting our soldiers killed while cutting their off-time and benefits, that the Democrats now, to me, actually do seem positively saintly. I suppose that is where the true inspiration for this originated. I think Bush has taken us so far off course that I practically agree with the bumper sticker I saw that said "Anyone but Bush." I don't think anyone else could do any worse. Iraq is now a giant hole that is sucking money and people out of our country where they are desperately needed. It's going to take forever for that unnecessary mess to be fixed and for us to regain the trust of the allies we've insulted by disregarding the will of the world community. All the while, I can't help but to think of the health care and education that the $100 billion we've spent (so far) in Iraq could have bought for Americans; or the millions of Iraqis who at least had electricity, running water, communication and civil order under Saddam Hussein. Life wasn't that great in Iraq before we attacked their country, but for millions of people, they were certainly better off than they are now. The Iraqi and Afghan people do not deserve what we have done to them. But at this point, perhaps I am falsely assuming you are a Republican, or at least planning to vote for Bush. I apologize if either is untrue.

Thanks again for writing and for being open to sharing our opposing views. As I've said to many others who have written, I think America needs more of what you and I are involved in right now; showing respect for other's opinions, especially if they differ from our own. We're all in this together and while we might not agree, we will be better off if we understand and accept each other's beliefs and recognize each other's right to believe whatever they want.

Best regards,
Scott Ritcher.

It was Mr. Artist, in the cloak room, with the candlestick

You say you went to Catholic school for 12 years. Where were you in class; in the cloak room hiding instead of learning about God AND Morals AND God's Word?

You say that the responses from Christians are very un-Christian-like. You expect us to all "Turn the other cheek?"

Well mr. artist, I expect you got your so-called artistic gift from satan, because God most certainly wouldn't ordain you to do such ridiculous work such as this.

Remember... we Christians are not angels so maybe we sometimes refrain from turning our cheeks after being smacked by idiots like yourself who is willing, like Clinton to prostitute yourself for money or what you may think as fame, whereas it is infamy instead & except for those of your same ilk, everyone is looking down on you with disgust!

You say you love God's creation so you are a vegetarian. This shows more of your ignorance; God put these animals on Earth for people, His main creations, for us to subdue these animals, fish & fowl & use, which included to eat as food, so mr. artist, don't try to sound so sweet & nice; you are instead showing your low-class stupidity!!!

—Jerry, earthlink.net

Jerry,

If you believe that God put animals on Earth for people "to subdue," that must mean you've been reading the Book of Genesis which also describes talking snakes and people who live longer than 500 years; but since you use the term "cloak room" it's possible that you actually are older than 500. You'll probably die soon anyway from high blood pressure the way you get all worked up over shit after eating all those Quarter Pounders. Where were you in school when they were teaching the detriments of run-on sentences? I hope you realize that now that your letter is in this book you may achieve what you may think as fame, whereas it is infamy instead and except for those of your same ilk, everyone is looking down on you in disgust.

- Scott Ritcher

P.S. Get bent, you old fucker!

You're going to go and build his ego up even more

Are you out of your mind, creating this so called art of Bill Clinton as God? After all of the bad (to put it mildly) things that he's done, you're going to go and build his ego up even more than it already is!!!!!

Whether you meant this to be funny and entertaining to people or not. And whether you did not mean for it to offend people, IT DID OFFEND US.

This man committed adultry, time and time again. With you doing this, you are making light of that fact.

—Mike, yahoo.com

Leaders that defy our own justice system

How dare you portray an adulterous, drug using, lying perjurer asshole as a Saint!

This truly shows just how pathetic of a society we have become when we continually glorify a dishonest cheat who was supposed to represent us and our country.

I personally do not like the fact that we look like an immoral country who rewards leaders that defy our own justice system. Wake up and realize just how ignorant these kind of cutesy portrayals make us look. Hell, Bundy was charismatic and people liked him too, maybe we should try to sell him over as a God. At least He didn't look like Mr. Magoo!

Just because Clinton didn't have the balls to go against the grain and only made decisions that were sure to win votes, didn't make him a great leader. Come to think of it though, he could have gotten away with anything so maybe he should have!

You people would have loved him even more!!!!!!! At least he would not have been such a coward.

I'm sure all of the service men of the past and present that died to defend our great nation would not have done so, willingly, for a leader whose own wife can't even trust him.

I'm embarrassed of what we have become.

Sincerely,
An American about to vomit
–Derek, ea.com

Derek,

I could discuss the ways we disagree for many days, but I'll simply say that I think you're wrong about a lot of things. As far as Clinton's alleged resemblance to Mr. Magoo, I would remind you that he looks just as God made him. I found it interesting that you capitalized "He" when referring to Ted Bundy. Leaders that defy our own justice system? Are you referring to Bush and Cheney's refusal to speak in public and on-the-record with the 9/11 Commission? Clinton didn't have the balls to go against the grain and only made decisions that were sure to win votes? I don't think allowing homosexuals in the military, instituting stricter welfare rules, or trying to stabilize Somalia were big vote magnets. The servicemen who died to defend our nation wouldn't have done so for a leader whose wife can't trust him? Maybe it's better to die while invading a country that didn't provoke the fight for a leader the United Nations can't trust. How is Bush any different than Saddam Hussein at this point? So, like him or not, at least Clinton held regular press conferences, let people ask him questions about policy and gave answers in a comprehensive way that left no doubt that he understood what he was being asked. That's more than can be said for Bush. After reading your letter and many others, I, too, am embarrassed of what we have become.

- Scott Ritcher

Lucifer Clinton

It should be saint Lucifer Clinton

—Bruce, comcast.net

Best idea since the pet rock

You are one smart artist. I wish you all the luck and success in this endeavor. I may disagree with President Clinton as a Saint, but this is the best idea since the pet rock. That is not meant as sarcasm or an insult.

—Professor Mark, maggard.us

Supposively... aweful... harsly...

I was reading the comments made by Ritcher, "oh wouldn't this be funny"... from the article 'Saint Bill Clinton' ignites religious rage. And since he decided to take his unintelligent stab at Christians for making comments against his product. His sense of humor is well documented in the Book he supposively was so well educated in for 12 years in the Catholic school. The exact thing he is doing is taught against. Or does he only believe in the parts of the Bible that fit his lifestyle? I'll stop now and let the reference speak for itself. Highlighted so there is no confusion for Scott.

Ephesians 5
3 But among you there must not be even a hint of sexual immorality, or of any kind of impurity, or of greed, because these are improper for God's holy people. 4 Nor should there be obscenity, foolish talk or coarse joking, which are out of place, but rather thanksgiving. 5 For of this you can be sure: No immoral, impure or greedy person--such a man is an idolater-- has any inheritance in the kingdom of Christ and of God.

There you see Scott the the standard for which the comments are made to you. Oh these aweful so-called radical Christians you speak so harsly against who simply try to steer you in the right direction.

–Craig, jacobs.com

His hucksterism is inherently evil

To Whom It May Concern,
Especially Scott Richter:
Re: _____ Clinton products.

I must admit to being continually more amazed and saddened when the boundaries of decency are violated in increasingly worse ways than before.

Mr. Richter's defense of his disgusting products would be laughable if it was not so blatantly arrogant and self-serving. Since he claims to have been raised Catholic, I don't believe it is necessary to explain why his art and his hucksterism is inherently evil.

I wish Mr. Richter no ill will. He will receive his just rewards at the proper time. I will leave that duty to God. However, I would not want to be in his shoes come judgment day. I do know that much.

For the Record: Yes, I am a Christian and a Catholic. Yes, I find the artwork, the products and Mr. Richter to be blasphemous, pathetic and disgusting.

—Kevin, earthlink.net

Kevin! How dare you attack my hucksterism! I consider this to be a hate crime against hucksters everywhere!

For every TV preacher... there are a hundred other... anti-Christian stations

Mr. Ritcher,

First of all let me say that I realize that your most recent work is probably intended to be humorous, but you must also realize that most people (myself among them) do not think that it is at all amusing or appropriate. You responded to your critics by quoting the widely known yet easily misunderstood verse "Judge not, lest ye be judged". When Christ said that he did not mean that we should just blindly accept everything that everyone does in fear of judging another person. Surely man cannot see the heart nor should he assume what the heart holds; this is what Christ did not want to happen. But we are to judge the actions and the fruits of the actions of other men. If not, what good is the law or government? Christ spoke out against the corruption of the religious leaders as well as the immorality of the people, so how can it be said that we should not oppose wrong-doing?

You also suggested that we as a country should turn the other cheek, in this statement I can only assume that you were referring to Afghanistan and Iraq. Again, you misunderstand the meaning of Christ. Yes, Christians are supposed to turn the other cheek when we face pursecution and when we are wronged, but governments and law enforcement are charged with the protection of the people who live under them and they cannot turn the other cheek. Many people think that God doesn't care about sin because he loves us, this is not the case. Though God does love us beyond anything that we can imagine, he also cannot abide sin nor can he allow it to go unpunished. This is why God sent his son so that he could pay the price of sin and those who choose can have their sin judged there on the cross by accepting the gift that Jesus is holding out to us.

I don't know how you can look at this society and see an imbalance on the side of Christians. When most of the media, Hollywood, and the society is pushing immorality, irresponsibility, and the attitude that there is no ultimate right or wrong, how can you say that Christian views are being forced upon you? For every TV preacher (many of whom do not teach true Christianity) there are a hundred other non-Christian and anti-Christian stations, and our plight is little better on the radio.

I truly hope and pray that you will consider the things that myself and others have said, and I am sorry if you have been offended by mean-spirited comments from those who call themselves Christians

Respectfully,
–Eric, pacbell.net

TOM, SISTER GENEVIEVE, SCOTT AND THE PIXEL DEBATE:

Scott,

I will be up front in saying that I am a practicising Catholic and that we clearly disagree on several issues. And I won't deny that you make several valid points about the failings of many Christians. I certainly am not immune from great personal failings.

And I in no way wish to deny you the right to disagree and to voice that disagreement. But the way you have chosen to express this is greatly offensive to me. Sickening even. Any practicising Catholic should recognize that you have used an image of the Sacred Heart of Jesus to make your image.

To those of us who believe, this is sacrilegious. Make Clinton a "normal" saint with a halo and I might not like it, and I might try to talk you out of it, but I wouldn't be insulted, offended and sickened by it.

In all honesty, can you say that you would you superimpse the face of "St. Bush" on a clearly recognized picture of Martin Luther King? Or Budah? Or Muhammed? Or one of Iraqs current well-known Imams? Or Gorbachev? Or Jacques Chirac? Or Gerhard Schroeder? And to add insult to injury, would you then produce products and sell them?

I hope you have the intellectual integrity to admit that you would not create or market any of the above "St. Bush" items - not even as you said "to amuse and entertain people." Why? Because you would realize that, intended or not, it would seriously offend people in a very significant and substantial manner.

And so if you would not offend these other people - regardless of whether or not you disagree with them on important issues -

why are you so willing and seemingly eager to offend those of the Catholic/Christian persuasion?

You cast some stones at Christians (and some of them hit their mark). But how are you any better than those you accuse when you show your own prejudice by deeply offending Catholics and Christians when you would not do so to other groups of people?

Scott, I do believe in Him whom you have defaced, and I will pray that you will find it within yourself to begin treating your Christian sisters and brothers with the same decency that you would treat anyone else on the face of this planet we call home.

–Tom, shentel.net

Dear Tom,

I feel I did not deface your God. I defaced a replica of an 18th Century painting of a white person who no more resembles Jesus than Ted Nugent. To me, the significance put into Catholic sacred imagery seems eerily akin to idolatry. It's a picture. It's not Jesus himself. The man in the picture isn't even dressed like a poor fisherman of the day would have dressed. He is dressed like a territorial, political king would be.

I just don't understand how certain arrangements of paint or pixels can be considered as an attack against a religious group. The small image here at the right is the same "Saint Clinton" image that has caused such outrage, but the pixels have been rearranged. Is it offensive now? Everything that made it "disgusting" and "sickening" is still there, but I have a feeling if this image was being discussed in newspapers it wouldn't have ignited the same firestorm.

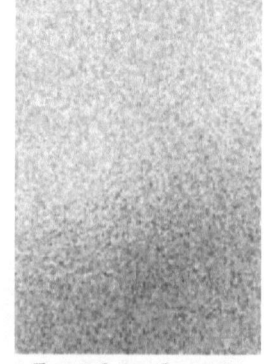

FIG. 4: SAINT CLINTON WITH PIXELS RANDOMIZED

Sure, if it was an image of a Catholic priest being sexually pleasured by a young altar boy, I could understand the anger. The extra irony here is that President Clinton is still demonized and called abhorrent as a result of sins for which he has confessed and asked forgiveness, while officials in the Catholic church have gone out of their way to protect themselves and criminal child molesters from prosecution, even at the cost of subjecting more innocent children to truly sickening and disgusting acts. That is to say, acts that are sickening and disgusting to people of any faith; even to atheists.

- Scott Ritcher

From your letter [above], I can see that you have no idea of the magnitude of what you did. Red white and blue, are just red, white and blue, until they are put together in a certain order to make a flag.... And even different flags at that, Russian, US, British, New Zealand, Austrailia, etc, etc. But deface one of them and the corresponding country will be appalled. Not because of the colors, but because of what those colors represent – their country! It is the same with this picture. Any Catholic should be offended personally by this. It is a "picture" of something that represents Someone very near and dear to them. It shows the power of "art". I ask you to please take these things out of circulation. Or you will regret it when you meet that Someone in eternity.

–Sister Genevieve, stmarys-parish.org

Having read some of the feedback, I am sure that is exactly what you want to hear: outrage. You wanted to create a sensation. Well I don't intend to give you that satisfaction. I hope the Sacred Heart will extend His suffering love even to you and make you understand what you have done to Him and to yourself. I will pray that you are converted and live long enough to make reparation for this sad blasphemy. When you see Him in eternity, you will want to see HIS face above the broken heart you caused. Please take your things out of circulation, and don't make that meeting worse. Sacred Heart of my Jesus, I believe in Thy love for me.

–Sister Genevieve, stmarys-parish.org

Scott,

I did not say you defaced God. Actually defacing God would be impossible for you to do. What I did say was that your picture is sacriligious (insulting and grossly irreverent toward what is held to be sacred) and that it was offensive to me and many people of faith.

I give you credit for at least attempting to answer my email. But the fact is you completely sidestepped the main points. Your argument that the picture is "just an arrangement of pixels" is really not worthy of a response. But if you really believe the two pictures are equivalent, then we can both satisfied! All you have to do is take the new version of the picturewith the rearranged pixels which you emailed me and sell/display it instead of the original version. If you decline to do this, you've defeated your own argument. And of course we both know you won't do that. Sadly, I fear that this demonstrates your lack of intellectual honesty and integrity - though you desperately make great effort to seem so. You claim to be answering my concerns with valid and legitimate reasoning - yet you yourself do not believe what you are saying.

And I am still waiting to see your "arrangement of pixels" that are not offensive or insulting of "Saint Bush" (or even "Saint Clinton") on the clearly recognizable body of Martin Luther King, Budah, Muhammed, one of Iraqs current well-known Imams, Gorbachev, Jacques Chirac, and/or Gerhard Schroeder?

And yes there is sarcasm in the next paragraph. And I ask your pardon for it. But it's hard not to be sarcastic when you can't demonstrate true integrity and intellectual honesty. Your supposed serious and sincere arguments, if valid, lead to the following ideas as viable products for your artistic abilities and for your online store. In reality, I know the following products would be offensive (as do you) and I would never want to see them actually produced.

But according to your logic and argument there is nothing wrong with them and you'd have no problem producing them for laughs.

So here goes . . . I've attached a few pictures that might be good starting points for your artistic abilities. You could replace Buddha's head with Clinton or Bush or the Pope - sure to be a big seller in India. I'm sure you could superimpose Bush or Clinton on the Gorbachev photos and add the trademark birthmark to their forehead so we'd all know who it was you were only joking about - it could be the first item in your new Russian web store. And I'm sure you could do wonderful things with the photos of MLK and Malcolm X - sure to be hot item in black neighborhoods. And you could put the pope on the picture of Martin Luther King - I'm sure that would be a big seller at the Lutheran bookstores. I'm sure you can come up with many other products to sell that are jokes of this nature since no one would find them offensive.

Finally you speak of Clinton still being demonized for sins that he has confessed and asked for forgiveness. And you counterpose Clinton with officials in the Catholic Church who are child molesters. Again, like the "arrangement of pixels" argument above, this argument is no real defense of your "St. Clinton" picture. In fact, it has not even one iota to do with the discussion at hand - Clinton's picture mockingly set on a well-known picture of Jesus Christ.

But since you bring it up . . . First of all, I am not going to justify the heinous crimes of any child molester. What they did was despicable and they have much to answer for to the God they claim to serve. And I would add that the same Catholics who would find Clinton despicable would also find these child molesters in the Church despicable. The only Catholics who might not find them despicable are the pedophiles themselves. And be careful of painting all Catholics with the brush of guilt of these child molesters as you seem to be doing. The Catholicism of these sex offenders in no way defines who they are. In fact I would argue that they are not Catholics at all - but that is another argument for another day.

But getting back to the broad brush you used to paint all Cathoics with . . . If all Catholics are guilty of these heinous crimes simply because they are Catholic and the perpetuators were Catholic, then . . . that same brush will paint other strokes . . . For these pedophiles are also Americans, men, and almost exclusively they are homosexual . . . Would you paint all these with the same brush of guilt simply because they happen to belong to a group that includes criminals of a disgusting nature?

And not getting back to you saying that many Catholics find Clinton despicable. The sexual crimes of Catholic clergy in no way lessens Clinton's faults. And he has asked for forgiveness only for the very few offenses that have been exposed in public and which he could not squirm out of. He may be sincere in "confessing" and asking forgiveness for what was already exposed after he could no longer deny that he "knew that woman". But after all his gyrations in trying to wiggle out of it, can you blame people who doubt his sincerity? And if anyone has enough sense to look beyond the white-washed reports of the news on the major media, there is so much more "smoke" surrounding Clinton that there must be several fires there somewhere. And not that it matters to the discussion at hand, but since you brought this up, has Clinton confessed and asked forgiveness to other offenses that are hidden from the world of those who unthinkingly rely on major media as their only source of truth?

I will close by asking you to please remove your Saint Clinton products. You are quick to point out the flaws of many Christians - including their lack of consideration of and charity towards others. Even if you sincerely can't see why so many of us find your products offensive, the fact is that we do. Would you be guilty of the same sins that you accuse us of? Or will you do the considerate and charitable thing and remove these products which truly offend so many?

—Tom, shentel.net

Too expensive to give as small keepsakes

Hello. I would LOVE to have a set of Saint Clinton pictures to send family and friends but I prefer the oval or rectangular shape. Unfortunately those shapes are too large and too expensive to give as small keepsakes. Is there any way you can make the sticker or magnets oval or rectangular? They are the perfect size but not shape. Thank you.

—Crystal, arusya.com

I am better off today than I ever have been

You have got to be shitting me! I am better off today than I ever have been! Why waste the money making anything that has anything to do with Clinton? Of course YOU will have some extra money by selling your little trinkets to a bunch of suckers that actually believe this man did anything for anyone other than himself. But, you can live with that, knock yourself out!

I don't think I want Clinton in my house. He would probably lie to me and screw my wife while I am at work then blame it on a loophole in the law.

—Scott, us.army.mil

The funniest thing in the world right now

Oh gollygoshgoddamn. Saint Clinton -- perfect. But the baby I heart Abortion t-shirt is the funniest thing in the world right now for me, this Tuesday morning, 2:30 am, in the year of our Lord Satan Bush 2004.

your radio friend,
—Bat, swagradio.org

I want to apologize for all those Christians who have found it necessary to attack you (or) An image isn't Christ Himself and you can do no real damage to Him

Dear Scott,

I'm a conservative Christian but I find your Saint Clinton art to be very funny. No offense meant, but I always found Clinton to be a joke and this image confirms that.

I want to apologize for all those Christians who have found it necessary to attack you because of this image. After all, an image isn't Christ Himself and you can do no real damage to Him. And besides, when Christians react the way some have it kind of proves your point, doesn't it?

Aside from being a Christian I am an award-winning artist (watercolor) and used to be an award-winning art director and graphic designer in advertising in the New York area. So I feel with these qualifications and that of my being a Christian I can speak to you with some authority. Oh, and I also have a BA in Biblical Literature.

I feel very sorry that you have such a bad impression of Christianity. Sure, there are a lot of hypocrites and hopefully I'm not one of them - although I know that I'm far from perfect. I don't try to force Christ down anyone's throat as I know that won't work. Most genuine Christians feel the same way. We offer what we believe in but we want people to decide for themselves. And for those who are searching for God we make information available. There are a number of good preachers on TV and radio who preach to everyone - not just unbelievers - and I can say that some have helped me tremendously. You see I've been fighting stage 3 ovarian cancer for the last 12 1/2 years and without some of these Christian programs I wouldn't have had access to preaching many times when I couldn't make it to church.

I believe in the freedom of all people to make their own choices as far as faith goes. However, I believe very strongly that accepting what Christ did on the cross is the only true way to go. See, you get to choose and I don't judge you for your choice. Only God has the right to judge.

One other thing is that you should check the Constitution a little more closely. Separation of Church and State isn't in there. Thomas Jefferson wrote about it in a letter to the Danbury Baptists, but he wrote only to reassure them that the State wouldn't interfere with their practice of religion. Not vice versa.

Let me give you some advice and you can take it if you want. Try not to be offended by what Christians are saying and doing. Be tolerant. After all, we Christians are being asked to be tolerant of an awful lot and feel that those who don't agree with us should do the same for us. So how about it?

—Debbie, worldnet.att.net

Debbie,

I wish everyone understood that speaking in an educated, cordial way is the best route to getting those with opposing viewpoints to appreciate where you're coming from. It also makes others more willing to accept your view as a reasonable one, even if they don't agree. Thank you.

- Scott Ritcher

Your talents are being used to tear down this society

I can understand where your inspiration comes from. After all, Clinton has been a big supporter for the National Endowment for the Arts. This helped used tax dollars to create the 'piss Christ' and the Blessed Virgin covered in pornography and dung. Both of these profane works of art are 'protected' by free speech. Perhaps, you can place your work of art in a jar of urine and be paid for this by the NEA.

The life of the unborn has diminishing value in this society. Bibs like yours advocating abortion lend your support to further their radical agenda.

With your newest assault on Catholics and Christians, you have chosen to take the easy way out. You are actively opposing everything you were taught in your childhood. No doubt, you feel that you are 'free' to do and go as you please. Of course, free will is a gift given by God and was meant to do his work here on earth. It could just as easily be used to do the work of the enemy. Your heart knows where you stand on this. Your 'rebellion' against your religious background is not 'freedom'. Rather, it is slavery as you must do opposite of what is right.

I pray that soon you will see that your talents are being used to tear down this society. I pray that you will learn to forgive those that have either hurt you or disappointed you causing you to feel angry at the Church and God. Once this change of heart occurs, your art will change also.

May you experience God's love. May you find forgiveness for those that have hurt you. May the Lord show you how you have hardened your heart against them. Then you will find peace.

Yours in Christ,
—Bob, westernu.edu

I realize the gross nature of your art is purposeful

Dear Mr. Ritcher,

I was wondering what sort of person/artist/designer could've created such vulgar displays, so it was with sincere interest that I read an article detailing your response the outrage your products have elicited.

The Bill Clinton thing is pretty sick, but only because Bill was such a self-serving, immoral, unethical man. I realize the gross nature of your art is purposeful because it is too silly adbsurd to be otherwise. BUT, the "I Love Abortion" bib is what helped me understand you best. Your comments about Christians and pluralism is astoundingly ignorant. In order to understand what constitutes a "very un-Christian manner," you must first have a balanced view of what a Christian manner is AND what it is not (i.e. - your one-sided gee-whiz-I-guess-nothing-is-knowably-just outlook). Funny that a Catholic who actually appreciates his good Catholic education finds it distasteful/loathsome that "so much of American domestic and foreign policy is created from a Christian morality-based standpoint."

Sorry, but I'm going to dismiss you as just another uneducated, dishonest artist.

Study harder,
–James, bells.com

Riled up

The only thing funnier than viewing St. Clinton is reading how riled up the papists are.

–Vince, earthlink.net

Do you think that Saddam Hussein's image on an American flag would be funny?

1. If you "borrow" or "steal" most of an image to make some kind of point, then misuse or mislabel the image, you can hardly call yourself an artist! What you "borrowed" were NOT the robes of a saint, but of the Lord Himself. You are, therefore, mislabeling Clinton as a saint - literally and figuratively.

2. Separation of Church and State does not mean removing religion from the public arena. It means the governance of the Church (or churches) and the governance are separate. This does NOT mean that a religious person has to shed his faith or values when he or she becomes politically active. The fact that life is a precious gift does not have to be a religious value. It can, in fact, be a political or ecological value - i.e. the destruction of a bald eagle's egg(s) is a criminal offense. It can also be a logical conclusion: If the egg of a bird is so precious that to destroy it is criminal, and nature shows us that human life is "higher" than animal life, then how

much more precious must be the egg of a human being!

3. Why not use your creativity to create something funny that does not require "using" people or "misusing" symbols? Would you think that Sadeem Hussein's image on an American flag would be funny?

4. The reason some Christians are becoming less Christian is because the atheistic and materialistic culture we Americans have created makes it very difficult to be truly Christian.

and 5. Christians are not suppose to be wimps! We can express our anger at something as outrageous as your products. Be assured of my prayers that this particular venture of yours is highly unsucessful.

—Pat, aol.com

Dear Pat,

Yes, I think Saddam Hussein's image on an American flag would be hilarious and just as inappropriate as American troops trying to run his country. Americans have put the Iraqi people through more hardship in the past year and a half than Saddam Hussein ever did. No wonder our nation is so hated in the world arena. It's not because we lack morals in our culture, it's because our government shows an arrogant lack of respect for the borders, sovereignty and cultures of other countries, and does so all the while invoking the name of God.

Secondly, I did not borrow the robes of the Lord. I borrowed the resemblance of an 18th Century painting of a white man who looked and dressed arguably different than Jesus.

Best regards,
- Scott Ritcher

Yeah yeah yeah

This is an outrage! To even suggest that Bill Clinton is a saint is a putdown on sanctity. To use the image of the Sacred Heart of Jesus is sacrilege!!

–Danna, coffey.com

Exquisite

Not only is the artwork exquisite, but it's absolutely hilarious! I'm certainly going to buy something with St. Clinton on it soon. Keep up the great and hilarious work!

–Todd, ashbean.com

Motivated me to start my "Christmas" shopping

"Morality is simply the attitude we adopt towards people whom we personally dislike". -Oscar Wilde.

Absolutely brilliant.

This feedback is a complete hoot - thank you for posting it. The most amusing part is people claiming you have no idea what art is, but boy did they take the time out to write you scathing email. Boy did they become passionate. "Saint Clinton" is the epitome of art.

Unfortunately, those wo are outraged are either to stupid or too humorless to ever understand that. Saint Clinton also makes a damn fine t-shirt. I think it will really compliment my 'Sacred Heart Of Elvis" tatoo on my bicep.

I will be ordering one for myself, and you have even motivated me to start my "Christmas" shopping.

Keep up the good work.

—April, hotmail.com

For a split second I chuckled

It is sick. And it is blasphemy. Other wise it would be hilareous. The instant I saw it my first thought was that it was meant to be a mockery of the liberals who worship Clinton as there god and at the same time a mockery of a denomonation of Christianity that lines there walls with graven images. For a split second I chuckled, then I noticed the blood spots on the hands depicting Clinton as Jesus. I wouldn't want to be you on judgement day. Get right while you can, Sir.

—Pat; Texas

I love it!

Hi!

As Chris Matthews ever so lovingly says on Hardball, "HA!" I love it! You've got some great stuff up for sale. I would buy some bumper stickers now, but my car is too plastered with the stickers of local and national Democratic politicians (Kerry-Edwards '04, mate!), so I'll have to wait til after the election to get some. Saint

Clinton - that's priceless. Good job, and I especially applaud your response from WorldNewDaily.com. I couldn't of put it better myself.

Here's an idea - paint a picture of Saint Kerry, healing the blind ;)

Keep it up,
- Katie, hotmail.com

The Bible states...

President Clinton has the right to have the Holy Ghost like anyone else and if he will yield himself to the Spirit of God he can have Salvation like anyone else,but on the other hand if people like him follow in the path that they are following I'm sure that God will reject them if and when they get to the pearly gates. The Bible states that a person must repent and be baptized every one of you in the Name of Jesus Christ for the remission of sins and ye shall receive the Gift of the Holy Ghost. ACTS 2:38

-unsigned, bellsouth.net

Finally, the first "not" joke of the 21st Century

Bad taste? Sophomoric? Blasphemes? Yes, each of those adjectives apply and so many more. If you had found a way to symbolize Clinton as some Muslim equivalent the evening news would have carried it. However you chose the group that the mainstream media will not protect, middle America, the God fearing average American. Not it wasn't funny. Yes, it was in extremely bad taste. And just think of how many Americans died so you would have the freedom necessary to insult so many people. I am sure they would be proud of what you chose to do with that freedom...... NOT!

By the way, your 15 minutes are up. Someone please queue the fat lady.

–K.S., knology.net

Is it worse lying about getting laid or lying in order to involve your nation in a war...? (or) Religion should be banned from American public life for the same reason that alcohol should not be allowed around alcoholics

I really love your page, and even more love the reactions to it. I really do think that they show it is probably right that religion should be banned from American public life for the same reason that alcohol should not be allowed around alcoholics. Americans just cannot handle religion. Look at Britain! We have an established church, but people don't go crazy because of it. Americans have no sense of proportion, no sense of humour. So Clinton got a few blow jobs in the Oval Office from someone who made a major campaign out of her attempt to give it to him, for reasons only she will understand although maybe it is possible to say that she was the ultimate groupie. He also lied about it, but is it worse lying about getting laid or lying in order to involve your nation in a war that kills thousands of people?

Nobody has yet tried to put Clinton on Mount Rushmore, which is more than you can say for the fans of Ronald Reagan. At least when you call Clinton a saint you are kidding.

I think that the key to Clinton's success is that he spent time at

Oxford. Yes, he and Kerry demonstrated against the war in Vietnam, and Clinton avoided serving, but Bush and Quayle and Chaney and the rest all supported the war when they avoided serving in it. They liked the war but just thought it was for people with less money and power to go die in it. Maybe this makes them patriots but I don't think so. As far as Clinton goes he was a big disappointment in many ways, but beats Bush by every yardstick.

−Christopher; United Kingdom

Shame on you!

Your "sense of humor" regarding the very tragic issue of abortion reflects ignorance and callousness. No matter what stance one may take on this issue, it is shocking to think that any decent person would purchase your sick product to make a "funny" statement about something so personally painful and full of consequences. Shame on you!

−Weg, earthlink.net

To promote the pro-death/abortion agenda

Re: Offensive Pro-Death/Abortion Baby Bibs

How very sad that some people think this is humor to go so far as to promote the pro-death/abortion agenda by using innocent babies as bill board for their own demise.

−Anna Mae, peoplepc.com

Your... products are sent from Hell!

Hey, your "I Love Abortion" (sick) products are sent from Hell! You must be from there to produce such products and to find it funny.

−Josie, ec.rr.com

Shouldn't you add an aborted corpse?

Yeah, ha ha there, Scott. But for the full effect, shouldn't you add an aborted corpse? Which would be more ironic, one torn into pieces by D&C, ripped apart by D&E, or fully formed with his or her skull crushed and brain removed by D&X? For the ultimate in irony, you should consider donating a skidload to each of the numerous organizations for grieving women who deeply regret their abortions and have suffered physically, emotionally, and spiritually because of them. I'm sure with your genius you can show them that it really is all a laughing matter.

Sense any irony there, Scott?
−John, sympatico.ca

You need to apologize to all America (or) "I'm discussed"

The " I love Abortion" products that you have created are in such bad taste that I think you need to apologize to all America. Death and celebrating killing is not an American quality to be desired. Shame on you for making America look cheap. I'm discussed

−Mary Ann, modempool.com

"Rediculous"

Scott, I learned today of new line of baby t-shirts that are just rediculous. "I love abortions" for babies? This falls in the category of "what were you thinking??" I doubt that you were. I sincerely hope that you are currently reconsidering this line of products and plan to end it at the soonest moment. Last time I checked, life and death matters were no joke. I'm sure the kids in your family look fantastic in them.

—Matt; Chicago, Illinois

So ignorant as to believe that women don't suffer deeply

Thank you for the "I Love Abortion" merchandise. It will evoke sympathy for those persons who are so ignorant as to believe that women don't suffer deeply from having an abortion. For those who counsel these grieving women, nothing else so perfectly illustrates the ignorance and cruelty of those who support the killing of defenseless children.

—Joe, norwichdiocese.org

Go straight to Hell

GO STRAIGHT TO HELL, DO NOT COLLECT YOUR $200!

—Ron, myexcel.com

Please don't teach theology

12 years in Catholic school? Wow! You surely missed the point. Please don't use the "turn the other cheek" as it's only Christian to be a door mat to evil. Please don't teach theology. You admit you're not a Christian. You have an opinion obviously... that's OK. Just don't teach your opinion as fact or faith. Read the Old Testament. God himself judges evil with terrible retribution. It's about love and the other side is sin and judgement. You can't one one without the other.

Oh well. Deaf ears.

Wish you enlightenment.
—Susan, amaisd.org

Occasions when man will let God down

This young man has only dishonored himself and his talent, which is a gift. He has mocked the one individual who gave the "ultimate gift" to save humankind. Being raised Catholic, he can not claim ignorance for what he has really done. Our Lord does not deserve the irreverence of such caustic humor - sad and childish as it is. As long as there is "free will," there will be occasions when man will let God down - and each other. Sadly, this is one of them.

—Valerie, incris.com

Yap yap yap yap yap

This is shameful! You have no respect for God or for people's religious beliefs. It is pathetic that there may be a market out there for this kind of stuff. When you are face to face with the Lord, I dont think you will find it so funny. His wounds on the cross were not meant to be a laughing matter!

—M.N., bethesda.med.navy.mil

A large majority of us don't want to see this perversion

You said you were raised a catholic, so how can you mock the saints that you were taught about in school like this. I also think that your abortion bib is a very sick idea. You complain about the religious programing on TV and radio, well what about all the sex, violence and filth that is all over the TV and radio. Do you think that it is all right to show this garbage to our children. A large majority of us don't want to see this perversion on TV but it is imposable to turn the TV on and not see this junk. You say you don't want to see our programing but it is only on a few channels where this other garbage is on every channel. As for war read your bible it is full of wars, all the nations of the world were always attacking Israel. Yes the bible says not to judge unjustly therefore I do not judge you. I do however judge your work and do not think there is anything remotely funny about it. MAY GOD HAVE MERCY ON YOU.

—John, earthlink.net

My life is great

I am sorry you feel that your life is worse off than it was 4 years ago at the hands of one man. My life is great, but I don't think it would have changed much, regardless of who is in office. Nothing happens by chance, and all events are predestined, no matter who the captain of the ship.

As far as your art goes, Christians will get upset by it because it is viewed as blasphemy. I am not apologizing for my fellow Christians, just saying that sometimes all of us at some time or another, will speak before thinking. Yes, we are not to judge, especially when beliefs are not the same. I am not judging you, and would hope the same from you, from some things I have read, I just needed to speak my peace, because everyone is so quick to bash each other. This country was founded on Godly principles, but everyone is free to believe and say whatever they want.

—unsigned, aol.com

A FEW ONE-LINERS:

Sir, I will pray for you as you are Lost.
—Deanne, sbcglobal.net

Probably the most desecrating thing I've ever seen. It aint funny McGee
—Jim, earthlink.net

I love it! These are great. I just made my order and I can't wait to get my stuff. Hysterical!!!
—Judi, aol.com

This is a joke right
—T.R.B., aetworld.com

Effing hilarious! Great work.
—Derek, unisys.com

Dear Mr. Ritcher: Your "Saint Clinton" image and products are an absolute sacrilege to the Sacred Heart of Jesus. Sincerely,
—Paul, comcast.net

Do me one favor

I couldn't agree with you more about how hypocritical us Christians are..we truly are. I apologize for that.

Christians aren't perfect they are just forgiven.

Do me one favor however..when you quote scripture to make a point stop taking it out of context and quote the whole or none at all.

Thanks and may God bless you,
—Pamela, aol.com

Complete ignorance of God's good grammar

I am absolutely OUTRAGED! Good Christians everywhere (and you are NOT one of them!) who read the Bible with great regularity, still live in complete ignorance of God's good GRAMMAR!! People!! Have you read these letters? The Lord hates it when you disregard the laws that He Himself devised when He wrote that Book! We are one holy, Catholic, and apostrophic church, remember?

—Paul, rcn.com

God will judge you appropriately

Unfortunately you reside in a country where you can exercise your first amendment rights. I wish I could express my true feelings without resorting to profanity but I am satisfied that our God will judge you appropriately.

If you really believe, how about Allah tees, mugs, lunch boxes, etc. in Saudi Arabia? But then again you only have one head.

IN GOD WE TRUST
—Cecil, mequiteweb.com

The reason for 9/11

You people are crazy.....................to think he was a good president just because the economy was good during his terms, His no action to all the bombing we had in the 90's is the reason for 9/11

—Wallace, bellsouth.net

You seem to be interested in the reasons for 9/11, so I thought you might like to know that its mastermind and the commission created by the victims' families agree on the cause: America's abrasive, arbitrary foreign policy.

"(Western nations) rip us of our wealth and of our resources and of our oil. ... They kill and murder our brothers. They compromise our honor and our dignity and dare we utter a single word of protest against the injustice, we are called terrorists.

"The United Nations' insistence to convict the victims and support the aggressors constitutes a serious precedence which shows the extent of injustice that has been allowed to take root...

"America has no shame. ... We believe that the worst thieves in the world today and the worst terrorists are the Americans. Nothing could stop (America) except perhaps retaliation in kind.

"American history does not distinguish between civilians and military, not even women and children. (Americans) are the ones who used bombs against Nagasaki. Can these bombs distinguish between infants and military? America does not have a religion that will prevent it from destroying all people. We do not have to differentiate between those dressed in military uniforms and civilians. As far as we are concerned, they are all targets...

This is my message to the American people: look for a serious government that looks out for (your) interests and does not attack others, their lands, or their honor."

(Osama bin Laden, May 1998, http://www.pbs.org/wgbh/pages/frontline/shows/binladen/who/interview.html)

And the view from the other side:

"The US government... should offer an example of moral leadership in the world, committed to treat people humanely, abide by the rule of law, and be generous and caring to our neighbors. America and Muslim friends can agree on respect for human dignity and opportunity. ... If we heed the views of thoughtful leaders in the Arab and Muslim world, a moderate consensus can be found."

(from "What to Do?: A Global Strategy," recommendations on steps the US can take to prevent future terrorist attacks, excerpted from The 9/11 Commission Report, page 376.)

-Scott Ritcher

A FEW MORE ONE-LINERS:

Offensive, disgusting, and blasphemous.
—Al, tampabay.rr.com

You people are disgusting
—Thomas & Dale, dejazzd.com

You're weird! Start saying prayers to be forgiven! If you are truly artistic, why kneel in scum? Rise up and hold yourself in God's blessing.
—unsigned, cs.com

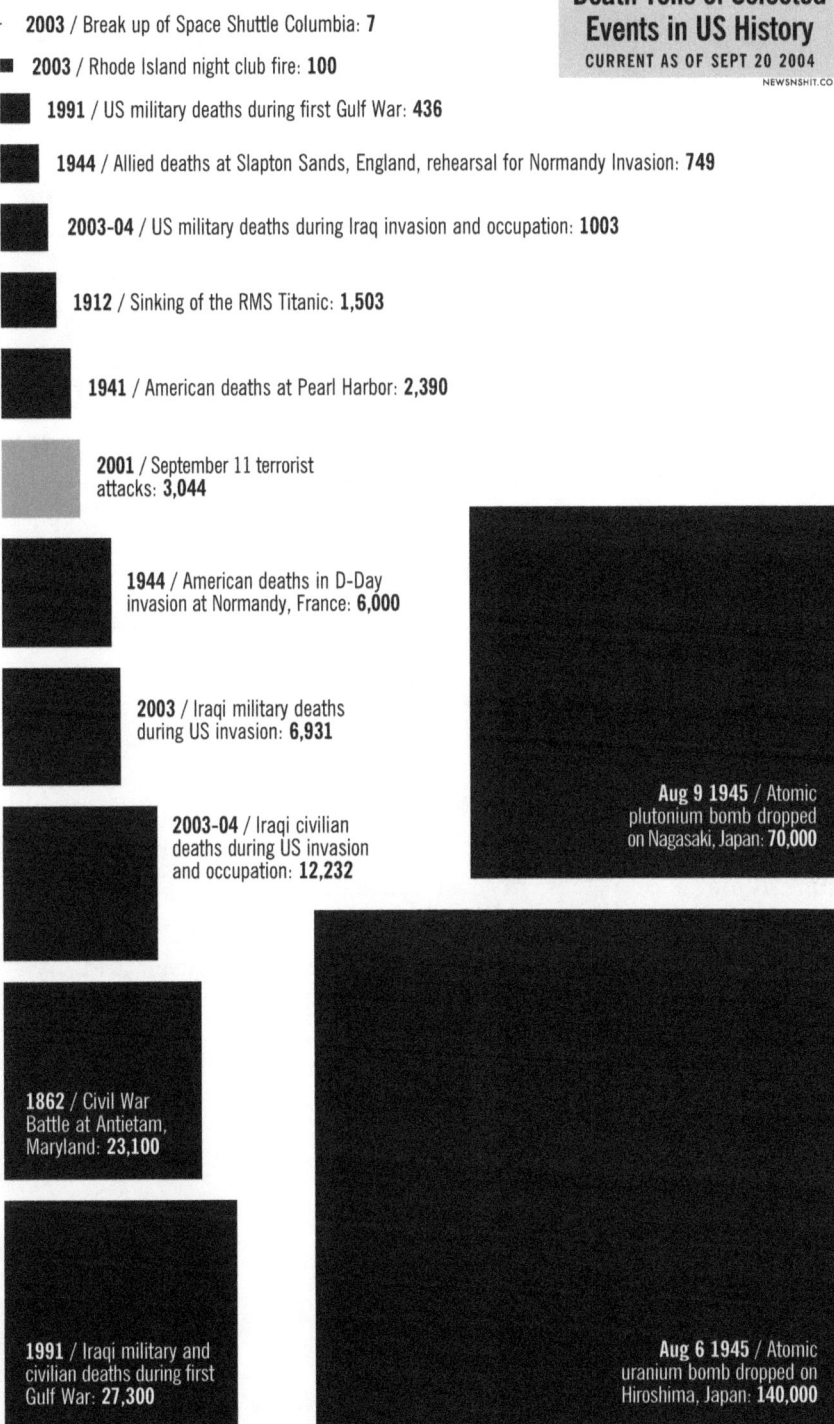

· 2003 / Break up of Space Shuttle Columbia: **7**

■ 2003 / Rhode Island night club fire: **100**

1991 / US military deaths during first Gulf War: **436**

1944 / Allied deaths at Slapton Sands, England, rehearsal for Normandy Invasion: **749**

2003-04 / US military deaths during Iraq invasion and occupation: **1003**

1912 / Sinking of the RMS Titanic: **1,503**

1941 / American deaths at Pearl Harbor: **2,390**

2001 / September 11 terrorist attacks: **3,044**

1944 / American deaths in D-Day invasion at Normandy, France: **6,000**

2003 / Iraqi military deaths during US invasion: **6,931**

2003-04 / Iraqi civilian deaths during US invasion and occupation: **12,232**

Aug 9 1945 / Atomic plutonium bomb dropped on Nagasaki, Japan: **70,000**

1862 / Civil War Battle at Antietam, Maryland: **23,100**

1991 / Iraqi military and civilian deaths during first Gulf War: **27,300**

Aug 6 1945 / Atomic uranium bomb dropped on Hiroshima, Japan: **140,000**

It's very sad that this is the state of the world today

Dear Sir,
I've looked at your product after seeing them on another website, and I must say I am very offended. Your remarks about the product and about the people who are upset about it are also offensive. As a Christian who ***does*** try to live a Christian life, this is poking fun at my God and my religious beliefs. I think that's wrong no matter which religion or which God you are talking about. Is Christianity the only one that will be the subject of your ridicule, or will you also include a line for Islam, Buddha, and any other religion that could be named??? It's very sad that this is the state of the world today.

−Sabrina, excite.com

There are too many nuts out there

I sent an e-mail a few minutes ago about your website, and I would like to request that *if* it happens to show up on your website, that my name or at least my last name be withheld. There are too many nuts out there for me to want my name on a public and controversial website. It's a matter of safety for myself and my family. I hope you will understand that whether or not you agree with my opinion about your artwork.

Thank you,
−Sabrina, excite.com

What did you expect?

You indicate surprise at reactions, but what did you expect when you take something you surely knew as sacrosanct and represent it with someone renowned publicly for immoral conduct?

You may not like Christianity's influence in our society in government in some ways, but it is what gave you the right to offend so many, and be proud of it. You wouldn't have that same freedom in Buddhist or Hindu Asia, or in Muslim countries. Sounds similar to "[hate] the hand that feeds you".

–Rich, microsoft.com

Christianity "has the greatest basis for truth" than do other religions

I read about your artwork in Worldnet daily, and I have to say I am far more put off by your understanding of Christianity than I am by your art. I don't like the painting, but I catagorize it with most of the empty election year hype surrounding us these days. However, for someone that claims to reject Christianity from a Christian perspective your understanding of the Bible is sadly deficient.

to the points you made:

Turning the other cheek has absolutely nothing to do with self-defense or war. We know this because two of the members of the twelve apostles carried swords - obviously with their master's approval. Rather, turning the other cheek has to do with recieving an insult, to the Jews of that day, slapping a person accross the cheek was one of the greatest insults you could give him. This comes from a misinterpretation of the Old Testament law by first century Jews. The civil penalties under the law was an eye for an eye; but it was to be carried out by the governing authorities. During Christ's day there were Jews who were using this passage to "take the law into their own hands" since the Jewish courts no longer had the power of capital punishment. By the way, Christians believe in capital punishment because the Old Testament law prescribed it (and "thou shalt not kill" would be better translated "thou shalt not murder"; the principle has never been taken to refer to a limit on civil government until the modern age. The Noahic covenant still applies: whosoever sheds man's blood, by man shall his blood be shed - and if he understands its wrong then no matter what his IQ the principle applies.

Niether does our Lord's teaching "Judge not lest ye be judged" has absolutely nothing to do with reaction against your artwork, nor have you been "judged" in the sense meant in that passage. The term judge has the idea of passing condemnation - no one has tried to kill you for blasphemy, imprison you, remove your right to vote, etc. They have as much right to protest your statement as you have to make it - that is not judging. In other passages Christians are encouraged to judge in the sense of declaring what God has said in His Holy word.

As for the rest, I think you need to study the issues of Separation of Church and state as well as logic more thoroughly. Logic dicates that not all philosophies or religions can be equally true or correct, otherwise we violate the law of contradiction. Either Christianity is true or Islam is true, or something else is true, but since their doctrines teach disparate truths all cannot be true. Yet when you look at the claims of Christianity it has the greatest basis for truth than do the others. Historically it has survived when it should not have; it has been villified more than any other religion on earth, it does not carry out the aggressiveness that Islam has had during its entire history, etc. Furthermore, your views of Separation seems to suggest we may be Christians at church buyt not in the voting booth. This suggests a trunciated idea of what religion is.

—Rev. Kevin, students.bju.edu

You might say

IHS
Dear reader,
Peace be with you. I rose this morning and offered my day to my
God through Jesus. I thank my Jewish Savior for His love and
His grace, and I offer Him my efforts on His behalf.

Which is why the merchandise you sell is offensive, even to
someone who enjoys irony and humor. To take an image of Christ
and distort it for profit is callous and careless. To an unbeliever,
the closest parallel might be distorting a picture of a loved one or
a parent, and holding it up for public ridicule.

Lighten up, you might say. I am. God is bigger, you might say.
He is. What calls forth a response from me is Love. And while
you may have the "right" to mock Love, that does not of itself
make it right.

Yours,
—Aron, franciscan.edu

Fear of the Lord

My only comments to a person who would think this was funny
or entertaining is this:

From the Book of Sirach; Chapter 1; vs 12 'The beginning of
Wisdom is fear of the Lord...."

You must not have any wisdom.

—Sabina, juno.com

DIALOGUE WITH UNSIGNED WRITER:

I HOPE YOU REALIZE THIS TRAVESTY TURNED OUR FAMILY FROM LIFE LONG DEMOCRATS INTO NEW AGE REPUBLICANS -

WHY DON'T YOU NOW MAKE A GRAND SLAM & INSULT JEWS, AFRICAN AMERICANS ,.MORMONS, LUTHERANS & EPICOPALIONS ?

I AM NOT EAILY SHOCKED BUT THIS PIECE OF CRAP TAKES THE CAKE!

—unsigned, aol.com

You don't get out of the house much, do you? I have never been a Democrat or Republican so I couldn't really give a shit if you switched from one to the other because of something I did. It's like telling me you switched from "Seinfeld" to "Everybody Loves Raymond" because something on "Cheers" offended you. If you're so shallow that something created by a person who isn't affiliated with the political parties changes your mind about how you feel, it sounds to me like you're bit of a flip-flopper. In the future, sign your name when you insult people as a result of your misinterpretation of what they're doing. As your newly adopted vice president would say, "Go fuck yourself."

- Scott Ritcher

You hit it right on the head I do not get out of the house much since my injury then stroke in line oif duty 10 years ago confines me to a wheelchair-sorry I was having a bad day-I apologize- I shoul have carried a bit of saity into my diatribe but the 8 meds I take each day to stay alive react in different ways on different days!

—unsigned, aol.com

Bodies being rent asunder (or) "Sodomy is sensational!"

Dear Mr. Richter,

While a tad puzzled over the defense that you've put forth for your "I love abortion" merchandise, which is "...intended to be humorous and ironic", it does give me another idea or two that you might wish to consider. My puzzlement is over the "humorous" part of babies bodies being rent asunder in utero, though I do see where you're coming from re the irony. Anyway, how about establishing a line of house furnishings, such as "Adolph's imported Israeli lampshades", or a line of "Sodomy is sensational!" adult diapers? These would seem to fit neatly your rather curious idea of comedic irony.

Sincerely,
–Frank, alphatech.com

Bible references as basis for practical arguments

For the record and to the author of this so called art; Jesus will judge the lost world, but he gave believer's authority to judge other people who say they believe. It's called church discipline. You can find the outline of it in the Gospel of Matthew and well as Paul's letter to Corinthians.

You're in the Jesus category.
–C.H., 711online.net

The last train to Caps Lock City

Are you a sick puppy or what? THIS IS THE MOST

SACRILEGIOUS OUTRAGE I HAVE EVER WITNESSED!
MAY GOD FORGIVE YOUR IGNORANCE.

–Barb, msn.com

OF COURSE THERE IS A DEFICIT, YOU NUMSKULL,
THERE IS A WAR ON OR IS YOUR HEAD STUCK IN THE
SAND? DUH!

–Barb, msn.com

My head is not stuck in the sand. The war is not the only cause of the deficit, but Bush's administration is the only cause of the war. Almost every country in the world warned the US not to go into Iraq, but our leaders were hellbent on starting an unprovoked war with a country that had not attacked us. Compare the current deficit to that during the two world wars if you think war is the reason for the shortfall. The Bush administration is irresponsible in nearly all matters of policy and fiscal accountability. And "may god forgive my ignorance"? Since when is a lack of knowledge sinful?

Scott Ritcher.

Jesus had a much better sense of humor

Hilarious! But here's my prayer: Dearest God, Please, please tell me that the losers who gave negative feedback to SaintClinton.com hoping that their blasphemous soul roast in H.E. Double Hockey Sticks is NOT indicative of the majority of voters on this very crucial voting year.

Plus, I think Jesus had a MUCH better sense of humor than most of these fundies give him credit for. He and Bill would have hung out, I am sure.

–Karen; Connecticut

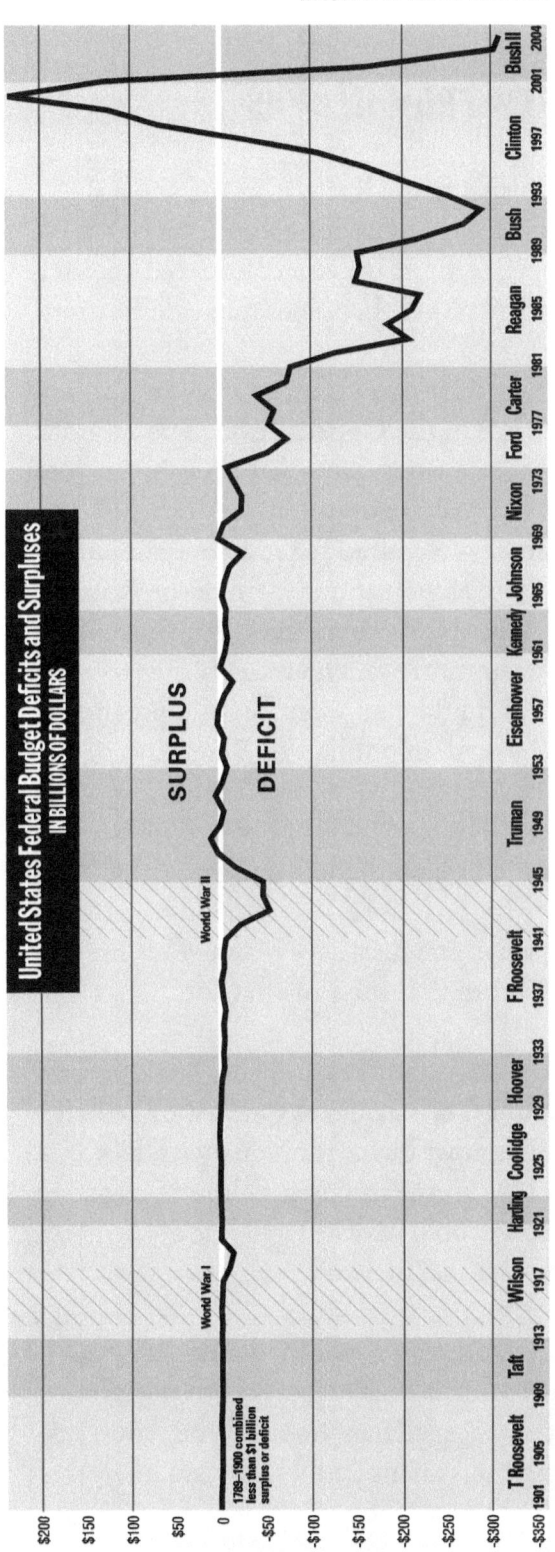

United States Federal Budget Deficits and Surpluses
IN BILLIONS OF DOLLARS

SURPLUS

DEFICIT

World War I

World War II

1788–1900 combined
less than $1 billion
surplus or deficit

$200 | $150 | $100 | $50 | 0 | -$50 | -$100 | -$150 | -$200 | -$250 | -$300 | -$350

| T Roosevelt | Taft | Wilson | Harding | Coolidge | Hoover | F Roosevelt | Truman | Eisenhower | Kennedy | Johnson | Nixon | Ford | Carter | Reagan | Bush | Clinton | BushII |
1901 1905 1909 1913 1917 1921 1925 1929 1933 1937 1941 1945 1949 1953 1957 1961 1965 1969 1973 1977 1981 1985 1989 1993 1997 2001 2004

BALANCED BUDGET: when the taxes the government collects is the same amount of money the government spends.

DEFICIT: when they spend more than they collect and have to borrow money to keep providing services. The deficit is an annual amount that is added to the debt.

NATIONAL DEBT: the total amount the government has borrowed over the years and still owes to other countries and banks. This number increases due to interest accumulation and when the annual deficit is added to it.

SURPLUS: when the government collects more than it spends.

When there is a SURPLUS, the government can use the extra money to pay back its DEBT faster. When people make less money they pay fewer taxes and the government collects less money.

WHEN GEORGE W. BUSH TOOK OFFICE IN 2001, HE INHERITED THE FIRST SURPLUS IN HALF A CENTURY. WITHIN TWO YEARS THE GOVERNMENT WAS RUNNING THE BIGGEST DEFICIT OF ANY NATION IN HISTORY.

In 2004, the administration planned to spend $1.16 for every dollar it collected. That was when they thought the mission in Iraq had been accomplished.

In 1992, Ross Perot noted that over 70% of the debt had been financed in short-term loans. The businessman warned the first President Bush, "That's suicide in business, that's suicide in your personal life, and that's suicide in your government."

G.W. Bush's irresponsible spending habits now seem to dwarf those of his father. The current amount of DEBT is greater than the amount of US currency in print, which gives the country a negative net worth.

SOURCE FOR DEFICIT FIGURES: WHITE HOUSE OFFICE OF MANAGEMENT & BUDGET. TEXT EXCERPTED FROM NEWSNSHIT.COM CURRENT EVENTS HOMEPAGE. PLEASE COPY THIS PAGE FOR YOUR FRIENDS.

DIALOGUE WITH ANDREW FROM ILLINOIS:

I guess it wouldn't be offensive to me if it was in the general "style" of a saint's portrait. I'm not Catholic, but isn't this a "pose" reserved for Jesus Himself? Have you considered creating more of a "saint" image of Bill rather than a complete deification?

Also, just one quick point: separation of church and state, as you may have already heard, is not in the Constitution. The original leaders of the 13 colonies were mostly Christian churchmen who fled religious persecution in their European homelands. What they were afraid of was the newly crafted federal government endorsing a denomination or religious house -- like the Roman Catholics, Episcopalians, Baptists, Presbyterians, Pentecostals, or Quakers. Their notion of separation bears no resemblance to what many believe -- that there should be no mention of God and no effort to "convert non-believers" in public life. That kind of suppression is the kind of persecution they were fleeing, and when I hear you talk in ways like, "The vast majority of people who do not share Catholic or other Christian beliefs must constantly sit by quietly and absorb – or try to ignore – the unending stream of preaching ..." I wonder what you may have planned for me and my family. Nothing good, from that kind of rhetoric.

I agree with you that modern Christianity is probably less Christian that Jesus would have it... but Christianity is defined by beliefs and actions -- both of which must be harmonious with His revealed Word to us. If you continue to flame public antagonism toward the beliefs, pretty soon you'll have less and less of Christian actions, which we already have too little of.

I'm interested to hear back from you if you'd like to dialogue. I don't believe I have bashed you. If I have, feel free to point out where I have. I'm saying this because I am hopeful you won't just try to bash me. You have obvious talent, and I'm always interested to talk with artistically talented people.

–Andrew; River Forest, Illinois

Hello Andrew,

Thanks for writing. As you can imagine, I have been flooded with emails lately, so I am considerably unable to respond to all of them, nor would I feel it would be productive in some cases. I decided to write back to you, however, because I really appreciate the civil, polite and educated way you addressed the issues.

I realize that what I've done is apprehensible to some people and yet wildly entertaining to others (including some Christians). I first want to say that I wish no one any ill will. I have nothing planned (as you put it) for you or your family. I sincerely feel, and to an ever more increasing level, that Christian people, especially the fervently devoted, are simply unable to see what life in America is like to those who don't share the same beliefs. Things that Christians do all the time are so very offensive to others, that I can't believe the reaction I've received at publishing what I consider to be a picture of something humorous. I believe in God, but (obviously) not in the sanctity or sacrilege associated with particular arrangements of paint or pixels. I feel the name and invocation of God is too often thrown around in a disrespectful way, and I understand that many people are as offended by my art as I am by slogans such as "God bless America" and "God bless our troops" - two blessings I feel God might be reluctant to issue. I can't imagine men shooting guns in another person's home are worthy of God's blessing.

I could go on and on. I really just wanted to thank you for being so respectful of my beliefs even though you do not agree with them. It would be nice if all the mail I've received could have been as respectful, sharing and inquisitive. That's what I think America should be more of; a respect for other's opinions, especially if they differ from our own. We're all in this together and while we might not agree, we will be better off if we understand and accept each other's beliefs and their right to believe whatever they want.

Best regards,
- Scott Ritcher

Dear Scott,

Wow! Thanks for writing back. I really appreciate it.

I imagine you have been flooded with all kinds of ungodly responses from people who say that they know Him. And yes, in beliefs, I probably am one of "them." So, maybe I can apologize for all "my" ignorant people – except the cross-burners; they have no part with Jesus' Gospel.

I admit to being a flag-waver, and singing "God Bless America" at the top of my lungs. However, this summer a sign in front of a small country church caught my eye, instead of "God Bless America" it said "America, Be Blessable." Most of that part of the country is fairly conservative and probably Christian, so I felt like it may as well have said "Christians in America, Be Blessable."

This past Sunday, I was in Columbus, Ohio, for the 40th anniversary of my home church (I attended there from high school through college). There was a short drama in the service about three guys who met for a morning Bible study, but just quickly prayed over their food, rated the Sunday sermon, and ignored their waitress who had obviously had a bad day – actually a bad life – and was hoping that one of these praying men would just talk to her. They didn't even tip her.

It was refreshing to hear my pastor say to the congregation, "Don't ever do that... ever, ever, ever..." And instead encourage loving action and big tips!

I share that with you to say that I am hopeful that there is an awakening among devoted Christians that is stirring up compassionate action to match beliefs and words. And I am hopeful that words said might be more carefully chosen and kinder. But my wife always says I'm too optimistic, so I guess we'll see.

Even though I believe that God lives inside of me through the Holy Spirit, I know that I'm far from perfect. None of "my people" are perfect... we're all human... good days, bad days, smart money people, always broke people, well-fed, needy, generous, grumpy, mad, lovely, and ugly, and no matter what, very imperfect. Sorry you're seeing lots of imperfection... I hope that you'll start seeing more of God in us -- love, joy, peace, patience, kindness, goodness, meekness, faith, and self-control.

Hope you have a great evening.
—Andrew; River Forest, Illinois

If you did this to a Muslim you would be marked for death

Frankly I view this as a hate crime targeting Catholics. Do this to the Jews or the Muslims and see what happens. Christians have turned the other cheek for too long. It's time to fight for your rights to believe in what you want to believe in without being attacked in this matter. This clown has taken one of Christianity's greatest image and put the face of a jackass on it. It would be like painting Swastikas on a synagogue. Now if you did this to a Muslim you would be marked for death. Bottom line Freedom of religion is a guarantee in America. You people have attacked this right and deserve to be charged.

—unsigned, earthlink.net

Fidel Castro... was raised in a well-to-do family

You were raised as a good Catholic? Sir, you are irreverent and immoral but certainly NOT an artist, don't delude yourself. You know, Fidel Castro, the cuban dictator, was raised in a well-to-do family. But the man's phyche was so skewed that he destroyed a country through his "love" of the Cuban people. You seem to share his depravity.

—Silvina, bellsouth.net

God bless American against scum like you

I think you are a sick atheistic skunk. Portraying a philanderer, adulterer and a pervert as a saintly figure shows what extent your deranged mind has sunk to. God bless America against scum like you.

—Rick, shaw.ca

Fess up!

Holy Moley!
You will sell a kazillion pieces of this art. I hate his guts, so I think it would be great to hang on my wall and throw darts at it !!! But I'll bet you hate him, too. Fess up!

—Nelly; Nashville, Tennessee

Funny as hell

Funny as hell, especially for a conservative non-christian. Thanks for the laugh.

—unsigned, charter.net

According to the bible, which hasn't had anything proven wrong in it yet...

It's one thing to not like somebody's faith. It's another thing to offend them because of it. I don't believe in Mormonism, Budism, Islam and a whole host of other beliefs, including the Catholic version of Christianity, but I wouldn't dare go out of my way to offend what is a deeply held religeous belief to someone. What you are doing is cruel and insensitive. Believe it or not, this country was founded on Christian beliefs. If you don't like the remaining, small as it may be, vestiges of Christianity in this country, then you need to go somewhere else.

I don't need to defend God. He's more than capable of doing that himself, as you will find at your demise. Just how do you think you're going to explain your artwork to Jesus? Guess what? He's real. And you're going to meet him someday. It's up to you to decide on what terms.

It's a big mistake to judge Christ by Christians. We will invariably let you down every time. We're human. If you can name one group of people that is perfect, you couldn't join them. Neither could I. When a person follows Christ, he doesn't become devine. We continue to be human. We continue to have human flaws. And non-Christians will be sure to point them out to us. But you know what? We've been forgiven for the things we've done. We're going to heaven. And according to the bible, which hasn't had anything proven wrong in it yet.....unless you have a relationship with Christ....you will be going somewhere else. Everyone lives forever. It's up to you, in this short life, to decide where you will spend eternity. It's not too late to change your mind.

—Max, charter.net

A FEW SHORTS:

Let me guess....You're gay too...
—David. ec.rr.com

You are as much a bigot as the "fundamentalists" you no doubt
despise. This may come as a shock to you, but bigotry works both
ways.
—Charles, yahoo.com

What a wonderful way to poke fun at the right wing zealots.
Compared to our current thief of the White House, Bill is a true
Saint. Thanks .
—Connie, bellsouth.net

I PITY ANYONE WHO MOCKS GOD IN ANY WAY
AS GOD IS A JEALOUS GOD OF HIS REPUTATION AND
HIS PEOPLE AND YOU CAN EXPECT GOD TO AVENGE
YOU FOR YOUR MOCKERY! YOU MADE YOUR BED
NOW YOU "WILL SLEEP IN IT".
—Eugene, comcast.net

Brilliant. Bloody brilliant.
—Phil, waveflux.net

Mr. Ritcher,
Even a person who has a pretty good sense of humor would find
this offensive; even non-catholics see the sacrilege here. It's a
shame that people stoop to "shocking" people to make money,
especially when it is against another's religion.
—Judy, bellsouth.net

I LOVE LOVE LOVE your Saint Clinton Goodies! Hilarious
and well done. As soon as I have some friggin cash for spending
on ME I'll be ordering the journal. Best,
—Yvonne, bathroomgirls.com

Another person bringing the Jews into this

Again, anti-Catholicism is the last acceptable form of discrimination... in this case "hate speech".

The "I love abortion" bib is even worse. Would you have Jewish people wear clothes saying "I love the gas chamber"? No one would think that was funny for very long, and for good reason.

–Dan, atchisonproducts.com

Barb from San Diego I

Oh, this so rocks! I LOL every time I see it!!! Have you told Air America Radio yet?

–Barb; San Diego, California

Barb from San Diego II

Hi Guy:
I went back and read the comments on your art. Some interesting, some thoughtful... most just pathetic.

I'd like to refer you to a commentary that I think may shed light on the two types of people that can be seen in your comments: Christians and Leviticans. The term "Levitican" was coined by John Scalzi on his blog at http://www.scalzi.com/whatever/ archives/2004_02.html, and I reprint his essay here.

FWIW I'd gone my entire 40 years of life believing that Christianity is a "religion" of hate and hypocrisy, dedicated to expunging all other religions and worldviews from the face of the Earth, a la the Inquisition, the extermination of the Caribbean Indians and the entire population of the south of France, and so on. Then I started reading the four Gospels (Matthew, Mark, Luke and John) and I was *astonished*. Here is Jesus, and most of what he is saying can be word-for-word applied to the hate-mongers spewing venom in his name. To the "godly" televangelist who was pulled over for driving erratically because he was reading porn on the highway. To the "godly" Bush and cronies who rake in the profits from Halliburton and their tax breaks, to store them up where moth and rust destroy. Oh, I could go on and on. Wolves in elephants' clothing indeed.

Suffice it to say, of all the people slamming you with Bible quotes, I didn't see a one from Jesus himself. It's all from the Old Testament, or from the johnny-come-lately Romans afterward, who took an early lead on exploiting Jesus for their own ends of male, and world, domination. Those humorless correspondents are Leviticans, for sure.

Well, I'm still not a Christian, because I'd be obliged to buy into all that OT crap about how gay men must be stoned to death, but women are not prohibited from lying with women, and a man is not prohibited from lying with his own daughter. To say nothing of Judges 19.

But I have a lot more respect for Jesus than I used to. And sympathy. Boy are those roaches exploiting him. (Him?)

—Barb; San Diego, California

A COUPLE BURNS:

Your party is despicable and disgusting and you will go to great

lengths to make this man a hero, when he was the most disgusting president we have ever had in the white house......!
–Ed, waukeshaengine.dresser.com

The writer erroneously assumes the artist is a Democrat.
⁓ Scott

The non-Democrat erroneously assumes that he is an artist.
–David, netscape.net

It is not too late for you

I will pray for you. To create an image of the President over the Sacred Heart of Jesus is nothing short of blasphemy.

It is not too late for you. Consider how your actions will be viewed by your Creator and Judge.

As said, I will pray for you.

–Robert; Centreville, Virginia

To God there is no separation of church and state

It saddens me that all God wants is for us to love Him. You were raised and educated Catholic, yet you seem to have no problem in wounding the heart of Jesus further. How can you take your religion so lightly? Don't you believe that we were all created to love and praise God? Do you think that's what you've done by putting any human's face on an image of our Lord?

Although man may say there's a separation of church and state, to God there is no separation. Your education must not have been

all that good. I'll pray for you and the vast majority of people
that do not love God the way He intended and the way He desires.

—Jackie, ureach.com

We have enough troubles to deal with

You are really an ignorant person. You must really have a warped
sense of reality and humor. Before responding to the responses
to your work, you really should go back to school. The separation
of church and state has nothing to do with acknowledging the
existence of a supreme being, but forcing a national religion,(oh,
kind of like the Middle East!!). And, turning the other cheek does
not mean to allow yourself to be beaten and/or killed. You
obviously did not learn anything in your 12 years of religious
education. Remember, an elementary knowledge of religion is no
match for a bachelor degree or better in other, worldly, subjects.
So get your knowledge of your religion of choice up to the same
intellectual level. In the mean time please don't subject our world
to any more of your so called, art" we have enough troubles to
deal with.

—Steve Boyle, diadenver.net

ANOTHER ROUND OF ONE-LINERS:

Please remove this display of 'hate speech' from this planet. I
thank you in advance,
—Jeff, cox.net

What, no holy cards? I need something for my wallet,
—Max, harvard.edu

Get a life!
—Karen, earthlink.net

When you produce toilet paper with his mug on it,let me
know,,,,,,,,,,,,,,,,
—Andy, charter.net

offer it as a roll of toilet paper and I'll buy.
—David, bellsouth.net

President Sleazebag's portrait would be appropriate on septic
tank covers, but as a Saint? You people have a very sick outlook
on life.
—Al, blomand.net

I'm a Christian (not of the Romanist persuasion) and I find it
very funny.
—Jeannine, earthlink.net

white trash do not attain Sainthood, husband or wife.
—unsigned, juno.com

All I can say to this is ...my goodness, it must be the end times.
—Dan; Sioux Falls, South Dakota

DeBussy understood that a work of art, or an effort to create
beauty, was always regarded by some people as a personal attack.
—Steve, verizon.net

You are a very ill person.
—C.H., adelphia.net

Wow, you guys are sick in the head. This website is proof that
liberals are certifiably insane.
—Marylee, aol.com

A baby bib that says "I love abortion"... priceless

I just read an article about your "merchandise"...what kind of sick, perverted....

heh heh

No, just kidding. I can't pull that off with a straight face. I think that what you've created is hysterical..."humorous and ironic", as you said. I think that the negative reaction you've received is unbelievable...I'm amazed at how people can miss the point so completely. A baby bib that says "I love abortion"...that's just priceless. Brilliant. I want to laugh every time I think about it. Irreverant, with the perfect splash of black humor.

Hee hee hee.

Keep up the good work,
—David; Atlanta, Georgia

Come to your senses

Do you really think that life is just about eating at nice restaurant, having a clean car or a day off. You really need a soul searching and shame on you for taking such a Sacred Image of Our Lord and desecrating it Praying that you will come to your senses
—Lisa, bellsouth.net

Only someone with no manners

Although you say this is intended to be humorous and ironic that doesn't mean that it isn't disrespectful, and in poor taste. It is in

very poor taste and insulting especially to Catholics as this is more
a Catholic symbol than a general Christian one. No matter what
you personally feel about Christians, and/or Catholics, only
someone with no manners would purposely, publicly, denigrate
a religion. Just because you think something is funny doesn't
mean it is appropriate and right to do.

—Linda, columbus.rr.com

72%

That picture is a piece of CRAP! He is the reason we are in this
fix now!!!!!!!
Saints dont seduce there freinds daughters in to Blowjobs!
Your obviously blind to the real truth of Americas perdicament!

—David, cox.net

Quotes, caps, exclamation points! This letter has it all!

OK ... you said we are not allowed to be angry at you mocking
our Lord Jesus? Well we are too, allowed to be angy at it!

Jesus Himself picked up a bull whip and beat up the people in
the temple ... who had turned the temple into a sleazy bargain
basement ...!

Maybe "sir" you should try a picture with a muslim; and then
you really would see wrath!!! ...What? You wouldn't do that to
a muslim because you know you cannot get away with the "trash
you call art" depicting a muslim!

Christians/Catholics are too allowed to be offended ! I am offended for them. And I do not like catholic graven images!

Christians are the only group I know who are not protected in this country ..And that is OK because Our Lord knows what you people really are ... No "sir"; we are not to JUDGE people's hearts, but we can JUDGE the FRUIT of your art! And is it is found to be crap from a bull!

Hope you enjoy your riches on earth !
—"His Remnant", comcast.net

I'm not screaming, my caps lock is stuck

GOOD MORNING,
MAY YOU BE AT PEACE WITH YOURSELF. MAY GOD
CARRY YOU IN THE PALM OF HIS HAND AND MAY
THE HOLY SPIRIT GUIDE YOUR TONGUE AND HELP
YOU TO SEE THE LIGHT. YOU WILL BE IN OUR
PRAYERS HOPING THAT GOD WILL CHANGE YOUR
BRAIN FROM MUSH TO THE LOVE AND LIGHT OF
JESUS CHRIST.
GOD BLESS YOU, SINCERELY,
—Catherine, msn.com

"The worse thing"

YOU HAVE LOST YOUR MIND! THAT IS THE WORSE
THING THAT ANYONE COULD DO TO THE IMAGE OF
JESUS CHRIST. I PRAY THAT YOU DO NOT HAVE
SUCCESS WITH THIS VENTURE.

—Joanna, aol.com

Using Bible verses to persuade a non-believer is like using gasoline to put out a campfire

Dear Mr. Ritcher:

After reading your tirade against Christians, I realized that you had left out some scripture quotes that are not quite as popular as the ones you used:

"The fool has said in his heart, [There is] no God." Psalms 53:1

"Woe unto them that call evil good, and good evil; that put darkness for light, and light for darkness. . . " Isaiah 5:20

"A fool's mind is like a broken jar – no knowledge can it hold. When an intelligent man hears words of wisdom, he approves them and adds to them; the wanton man hears them with scorn and casts them behind his back." Sirach 21:14-15

"Therefore no one who utters wicked things can go unnoticed, nor will chastising condemnation pass him by. For the devices of the wicked man shall be scrutinized and the sound of his words shall reach the Lord for the chastisement of his transgressions" Wisdom 1:8-9

"The fear of the Lord is the beginning of knowledge; wisdom and instructions fools despise." Proverbs 1:7

"For the perverse man is an abomination to the Lord. . . Toward the scorners He is scornful, the wise will inherit honor, but fools get disgrace." Proverbs 3:32-35

I'm sorry you don't want to hear anything Christian, but you see we are called to speak out, regardless of the price:

"Now who is there to harm you if you are zealous for what is right?" 1 Peter 4:13

"The faithful should bear witness to the Lord's name by confessing the faith without giving way to fear. . . (Catechism of the Catholic Church CC2145)

"If the world hates you, realize that it hated me first." John 15: 18

It sounds a little bleak at this point, but there is hope and there is mercy. However, God shows mercy only to the humble of heart, the poor of spirit, the repentant soul:

"My soul proclaims the greatness of the Lord. He has shown might with his arm, dispersed the arrogant of mind and heart. He has thrown down the rulers from their thrones and lifted up the lowly. The hungry he has filled with good things; the rich he has sent away empty. " Luke 1:46-53

"A bruised reed he will not break, a smoldering wick he will not quench. . . " Matthew 12:20

"Create in me a clean heart, O God; and renew a right spirit within me." Psalms 51:10

"For you do not desire sacrifice; a burnt offering you would not accept. My sacrifice, God, is a broken spirit; God, do not spurn a broken, humbled heart." Psalms 51:18-19

"Believing is possible only by grace and the interior helps of the Holy Spirit. But it is no less true that believing is an authentically human act. Trusting in God and cleaving to the truths He has revealed are contrary neither to human freedom nor to human reason. . . " (Catechism of the Catholic Church CC154)

So, how do you acquire a broken, humbled heart? Start by reading Psalm 22 and Psalm 23. Read all the Gospels, especially the accounts of Christ's passion. As noted above, the wisdom books are great: Proverbs, Sirach, Wisdom, Psalms.

It sounds like you were raised Catholic. For an explanation of the Catholic faith beyond that of an 8 year old's understanding, you can read "A Faith for Grownups", Robert P. Lockwood. I would urge you to take to heart the words of the writer to the Hebrews:

"For if we sin deliberately after receiving the knowledge of the truth, there no longer remains a sacrifice for sins, but a fearful prospect of judgement, and a fury of fire which will consume the adversaries." Hebrews 10:26

Sincerely,
–Paula, polysteel.com

P.S. For some facts about the Christian beliefs of this country's founding fathers and our Christian heritage in America you can go to wallbuilders.com. It is interesting to note that the constitutions of every one of the 50 states begins with some mention of God or a Supreme Creator. This IS a Christian nation, God help us if we lose sight of that!

Paula, Even after being made aware of the fact that their constant spreading of the Word alienates others, why are Christians so insistent to claim that this is a Christian nation? How can a nation with freedom of religion be a Christian nation? - Scott

This kind of tacky stuff is very popular

Just goes to prove that some people will do anything for a buck.

I would hope that no one would buy any of your stuff and teach you a lesson, but we all know that common sense and good taste are in very short supply among many people who consider themselves "artsie" right now. We also know that this kind of tacky stuff is very popular with those who share that lack of good taste. Thank God there are still a few professional and ethical real artists out there who are willing to wait for high pay in order to not compise their talent and their work. Unfortunately for you, you will never be know as one of them now.

—Jancy. bresnan.net

Wicked wretch, you are to die

Dear Sir,

I find this artwork if you want to call it that offensive and disgusting. This is a sacrilege against God and I hope you will soon realize how you are offending Him and acknowledge your sin and repent. Something like abortion should not even be joked about like you claim to be doing by making those I Love abortion bumper stickers, etc. You said that Christianity in general is becoming increasingly less Christian, and yes there are many false Christians in this world, lost christians, lukewarm Christians, and that is our sinfulness that has caused all of these things.
You do seem to be confused about what judging is, it amazes me how everyone says that when Christians try to lead others to the Truth which is Jesus Christ and try to guide them they call it judging or say we are forcing our beliefs on them. Since you grew up Christian and I don't know if you still consider yourself a Christian or not, you may want to refer to Ezekiel chpt 33:7-9 "Son of man, I have appointed you as sentry to the House of Israel. When you hear a word from my mouth, warn them in my name. If i say to a wicked man: Wicked wretch, you are to die, and you do not speak to warn the wicked man to renounce his

ways, then he sahll die for his sin, but I will hold you responsible
for his death. If however, you do warn a wicked man to renounce
his ways and repent and he does not repent, then he shall die for
his sin, but you yourself will have saved your life."
So, it is called guidance to tell others about the Gospel and lead
them to live upright lives. What Friend would watch another
friend walk right over an edge of a cliff and not warn him? And
tolerance is not letting people do whatever they want, that is
permisiveness and it is not love. You are right when you say the
war is wrong, what this country needs to do is to repent and fast
and turn back to God and He will protect us again. So, let us
show the world what Christ taught us, which is Love, and I will
have to say by mocking Him like you are doing with your "art"
is not love and will not help to show others what Christ wanted
us to show the world which is compassion, unity, love.

I will pray for you, my brother in Christ

In Christ,
—Angela, comcast.net

Is there anything as beautiful as this sunset?

Why don't you try and open your heart to The Truth? Have you
ever opened your heart to anyone? Open it to Him and feel the
warmth of His Love enter in! His Love is total and everlasting. You
really have no idea what you are missing. Just as He created the
world - so too, He created you! Remember that beautiful sunset
you saw the other day? You said to yourself, "Is there anything
as beautiful as this sunset?" God gently touched your heart and
answered, "Yes, you!"

—Carolyn; Massachusetts

SHORTS:

It is one thing to express one's political beliefs - pitiful as they may be - but to blaspheme is inexcusable. God is merciful, so maybe He can forgive you. I can't.
—Ed, worldnet.att.net

"Saint Clinton" products are blasphemous and a great offense to all Christians, and Catholics in particular. There is no humor in it at all.
—unsigned, aol.com

I believe You are a very sick person, I will be praying for you! You be so bold to put a true picture of an aborted baby on your tee shirt,,,,Thats what you are saying , is that you Love the act of killing innocent,,,what makes you any different that a terriost?
—unsigned, aol.com

just how stupid are you? i'm sure you are a gay man. mayb you burn in hell you weirdo!
—Christine, comcast.net

The extent to which an artist will go because of inspiration is not an excuse to ridicule or disparage a religous saint or icon. This is an affront to a specific religous group. Can we call this racial discrimination at the least. I'm sure the artist must have some sense of decency.
—Charles; Warren, New Jersey

Dear Artiste, What's the fuss. I've been worshiping Clinton since his second coming. He is God isn't he. I mean, didn't the millennium start when he became president? Aren't we in the midst of it now? Come on, folks. Did you miss the arrival of God? Worshipfully,
—Saint Pedee, swbell.net

Much thanks to President Bush's tax cuts

Blasphemy!

And, for your information, we now have more money to eat at a nice restaurant (which we did a few days ago), get the car washed (which we just did this morning), and take a day off from work because I am now my own boss. No thanks to Clinton's oppressive taxes--and much thanks to President Bush's tax cuts to our middle class--5 figure income.

We are not Catholic, but this kind of blasphemy is highly offensive to any Christian.

–Bud & Jan; Canmer, Kentucky

Our country was not better off four years ago

I am deeply offended that you dare to insult Our Lord Jesus Christ in this blasphemous "collection" . It belongs in the garbage where Mr. Clinton also belongs. Our country was NOT better off four years ago. We are a corrupt no longer Christian society. Until we turn back to Jesus Christ and the One Holy Catholic Chuch He established there is no hope for our country or the world for that matter. You would be better served by getting down on your knees and begging forgiveness from the Most Sacred Heart of Jesus who will not be mocked for much longer. The world will pay for it's sins with a severe chastisement. That punishment has already begun with us having to be led by such poor examples as your Mr. Clinton.In fact while you pray for mercy on your own soul you would be wise to pray for him too.

–unsigned, aol.com

President Clinton was a fine man

I think this is terrible, I think president Clinton was a fine man, I care nothing about his moral issues, but he did a tremendous job as our president and I would vote for him today to be President again, but the Sainthood is exceptional people into the Sainthood, I suppose next it will be G. W. Bush?

—Dolores, aol.com

Again, abortion and the Holocaust are compared

Maybe since you don't really think that people should be offended by your artwork you should also be diverse and create a bib for Jewish babies that says "I love the Holocaust" and a picture of Hitler in Moses' body. Do you actually use your brain to think? I think that they would be offended as well by that type of artwork.
—Antonio, yahoo.com

Or better yet, maybe you could put George Bush's head on Mohammed's body and sell it to Muslims, I'm certain that they would love to buy your art.
—Antonio, yahoo.com

Your little tribute to your own lack of talent

Mr. Ritcher:

I read the WorldNetDaily article about your little tribute to your own lack of talent and imagination. I would respond to every one of the ridiculous points you made, which consisted simply of repeating left-wing platitudes, but if you don't even understand the true meaning of "turn the other cheek," then your Catholic education wasn't as well-rounded as you fancy and I cannot help you.

I will mention, however, then you may be able to fool all of the people some of the time and some of the people all of the time, but you don't fool me. You claim that you didn't realize what kind of an uproar your garbage would create and that many would take offense at it. Really? Well, then either you're a complete moron or a liar. I suspect, though, that it's the latter. After all, you claim that you didn't understand what the consequences would be, but yet you also claim to be able to recognize "un-Christian" behavior when you encounter it. It's very interesting how liberals like you will swear six ways to Friday that you have absolutely NO idea what would offend Christians, yet then become an authority on Christian behavior in the next breath.

Anyway, you need not worry because I won't be writing a piece about you. You see, Scotty boy, I know that you're a publicity whore, so I wouldn't facilitate your desire for fame and fortune by giving you traffic and attention. Weasels like you should be withered on the vine.

—Selwyn, aol.com

Blah blah blah blah

As a Roman Catholic,

I strongly object to your selling this blasphemous material on your website.

—unsigned, wapda.com

I hope you like hot summers

Dear Sirs:
Thanks for proving beyond a reasonable doubt that Bill Clinton is indeed the AntiChrist prophesied in Revelation 13. Only the AntiChrist would desecrate the Sacred Heart of Jesus as your image of Bill Clinton has done.

I hope you like hot summers, because summer where you are spending eternity is year-round and even hotter than summer in Texas where I live.

Sincerely
–Michael, yahoo.com>

Does your mother live? Imagine her pain if she is reading what others are writing to you.

Dear Scott,

I find your "art" very insulting to the Sacred Heart of Jesus, Who has only shown you and I love, true sacrificing love.

To tell you the truth, I have felt very upset with what you call "art" regarding Clinton and our Lord.

Since you were reaised Catholic, you are aware that we believe in eternal life. This earthly life is just a passage to the other side. We will not take any goods with us, except for the good deeds we do for others, and the honor we give the Sacred Heart of Jesus, the Good Shepherd.

Eternal Life always helps me put my life in perspective. Are my actions gaining Eternal Life for me? Or will I spend some time in Purgatory, or go to Hell??? Certainly you might want to consider this yourself.

Yes, you were raised Catholic. You might not be a practicing Catholic at this time, but like it or not, you will ALWAYS be Catholic. You have been baptized and put on "Christ", His Light. The very moment you were baptized, Christ entered into your soul. How do you think Jesus feels with this piece you have created? Where are your god parents at this time? Mine are dead, in fact, they died when I was very young.

May the Sacred Heart of Jesus, the Good Shepherd, have mercy on your soul. If He comes knocking at the door of your heart, please open. He is a Gentleman and will never impose on you. However, He must be very saddened at this time. He does live, you know. He is Risen! I like to celebrate Easter and Christmas year round. "Our Redeemer Liveth"! Oh, how I love this song in honor of our adorable sweet Lord.

Scott, remember, NO ONE love you the way Jesus loves you. He loves you to the point where He gave His very own Life on the Cross to show it and save you, as well as me.

Come back to the Church, Scott. He is calling you by name. The Good Shepherd is calling you by name! He knows your every thought and feelings, He knows you since the minute He fashioned you in your mother's womb.

I am sorry for those who have been harsh to you in His Name. Please try to understand. How would you feel if we insulted someone YOU loved deearly and with all your heart and soul? That is what we feel you have done to the Sacred Heart of Jesus.

Please re-consider your viewing on October 1st, the first Friday of the Month. Does your mother live? Imagine her pain if she is reading what others are writing to you. Imagine the pains of the Virgin Mary in seeing a picture of Her Son modified as you have done.

I will keep you in my prayers, Scott.

Your sister in Christ,
—Faith, yahoo.com

Issue an apology

This is an outrageous, blasphemous image. It is an offense to Our Lord, and to all who believe in Him. Kindly retract it, remove it from sale, and issue an apology on your web site and in the press. Thank you.

—Colleen, earthlink.net

The Sacred Heart of Jesus should never be doctored with

As a Catholic who has a devotion to the Sacred Heart of Jesus and the Immaculate Heart of Mary, I am very offended by the image you have created at and request that you remove it immediately. What you have done by doctoring with a blessed image of the Sacred Heart of Jesus is blaspemy. Not only have you managed to offend many of my fellow Catholics with this image, but also other Christians and also the Sacred Heart of Jesus Himself.

Please, the Sacred Heart of Jesus is very dear to us and it should be respected and honored. It should NEVER be doctored to be made an idol of someone else, to be made in fun, to be riduled, or fooled around with. NEVER!

I realize you are a graphic designer so allow me to make this plea to your hopefully code of ethics. I ask you, don't you have better things to do with your time and talent than doctor with another work of art? Surely in your field it is frowned upon to take other works of art and try to make them your own by doctoring with them? I am sure with your years of experience, your talent, and creativity if you sat down and really took the time to explore, you could think of better ways to express your creativity, your sense of humor, and your talent by creating your own unique images and designs that would give you the respect and attention you're looking for by your peers and in your field.

Again, I plea to your code of ethics and your sense of decency and request that you please remove this image from your website.

Thank you very much.

May God Bless you.
—Maria; Massachusetts

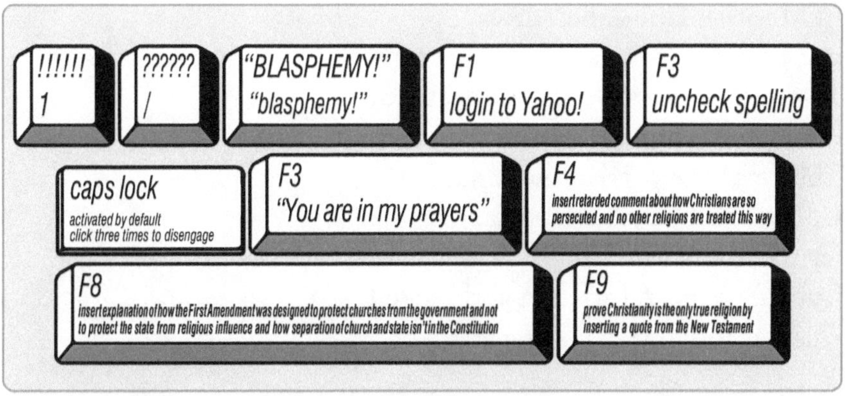

FIG. 7: PROPOSED SPECIALTY KEYS ON A NEW COMPUTER
KEYBOARD WHICH COULD BE MARKETED TO ANGRY CHRISTIANS.

No time for punctuation or capital letters

wow what an amazing idea keep up the good work i will often be reminded of the ecconomic prosperity and general well being of our wonderful country during those blissful clinton years through your great line of products

—Steve, bellsouth.net

In a world...

It is interesting how in a world where everyone speaks about the rights of people, animals, trees and bacteria no one seems to speak about the rights of God. Your blasphemy can only bring down God's wrath upon this already troubled world.
—B.W., aol.com

Rueben

Our faith was strong in th'Orient,
It ruled in all of Asia,
In Moorish lands and Africa.
But now for us these lands are gone
T'would even grieve the hardest stone....
Four sisters of our Church you find,
They'e of the patriarchic kind:
Constantinople, Alexandria,
Jerusalem, Antiochia.
But they'e been forfeited and sacked
And soon the head will be attacked.

—Rueben, yahoo.com

We cannot even pray any more in our schools

Blasphemy is the most serious sin of all, and if you were, indeed, raised Catholic, you would know this. I urge you in the most extreme way to get these blasphemous items off your website and use your art in a positive way that actually could help people.

You talk about being offended by Catholic or Christian images that have been bombarding the public. I disagree with you. Every day, most of the images we are bombarded with are totally secular in nature (look at ads in magazines, newspapers, billboards, commercials, tv shows, movies, etc.), and even the slightest mention of God or Jesus brings chastisement to those who promote anything Christian in nature. We cannot even pray any more in our schools.

Go to a private place, think about what you have done, and then, get rid of these offensive items. Use the talent God gave you to help people, not divide them. There is, and has been for too long, too much division among us.

Thanks for listening.
—unsigned, aol.com

The Lord put a person in my life who suffered as I did

Hello,

I read your post about the irony of "I love abortion" and "St. Clinton" items.

I want to speak to you about your Catholicism...I'm a Catholic that had to come back to the truth of the Faith. I went to Catholic school from K-6 and learned very little. I take it that you are young (say less than 50 LOL) and you are going for shock factor.

I agree with you that "tolerance" in the original sense of the word is lacking in today's day and age. But, you too must understand that as Christians (esp Catholics) we have had our God given freedoms taken and abused. The "left" is pushing their agenda's viciously.

Instead of say, a Creche', a Menorah, and a Star and Cresent, Santa with Reindeer to cover all the bases in public Christmas displays, we are PROHIBITED from seeing the meaning of the word CHRISTmas in the public squares. Many have gone so far as not allowing PRIVATE individuals from having religious images on their lawns.

This is only one example of the "Separation of Church and State". BTW, the actual meaning of that is not to allow an actual Nationwide Religion that is IMPOSED by the State. Say the President is Moslem...he says you are Moslem or ELSE! That's why the founding fathers but this in place. Not the way that the left wing media puts it.

Can you now see why Christians of all denominations feel threatened by your work?

Personally, I too find it offensive as NO ONE should hold that body except Our Lord and I had an abortion yrs before my conversion back to the beauty of our Faith, so anything that says "I love abortion" esp on a baby's bib! is mocking to the many women (and families) that suffered and continue to suffer the effects of the abortion. Mind you the physical effects are terrible at times but, the spiritual and emotional is far worse! Some women will NEVER recover from those...torturing themselves for the rest of their lives! I was lucky...the Lord put a person in my life who suffered as I did. She helped me to help myself.

Now I said that I would talk about Your Catholic Faith...I feel that you truly do love the Lord and wish not to blaspheme Him. If you are not still a Christian, that still doesn't mean that you couldn't come back to Him. I wouldn't have taken my time (hard with 4 children!) to talk to you if I felt you were a God hater....

I'm willing to bet that you (like I) never felt that there was anything "to" the Faith. I was a Cafeteria Catholic for a great many yrs. I was brought back to the Faith through a conversion. It was after my decision to come back to the Church that the Lord inspired me to LEARN my Faith. I'm blessed to be able to pass a Living Faith onto my children instead of the "Because I said so" type of Catholicism of years past.

Our Faith is so Rich...even in these days of scandal and discord...we still have the most important treasure there is...Jesus in the Most Holy Eucharist. Men are men and even in the early Church there was Judases. If one were to only view the priests and bishops that cause scandal (as well as whatever personal stories we all have, I've learned most fallen away Catholics have that same reason!)...then one would concede that we are all evil. However, if you sought out those Authentic Catholics who TRULY LIVE the Faith and viewed the Holy Father and learned the True teachings of this One Holy Apostolic Church, you would find the treasures I spoke of.

If you are in the slightest way interested in what I have said, feel free to email me back.

I'd be happy to help you learn more.

–Lori, yahoo.com

QUICKIES:

SHAME!! This is terribly insulting!!!! This mocks our precious faith and even more makes a mockery of our Lord Jesus Christ Please repent of this travesty-and soon! May Almighty God show His mercy towards those who mock Him!
—Rob, peoplepc.com

You people mock of the Catholic faith because you know the weekness of many catholics. Try to insinuate something against the Moslamism if you are a courageous man.
—Francisco, hotmail.com

there is no art in this . it is in very poor taste. shameful to say the least.
—Bob, comcast.net

While this is a humorous idea to "canonize" former Pres. Clinton, the artist should have used another image without the sacred heart of Jesus Christ. This is very offensive to me.
—Donald, comcast.net

This is the most disgusting piece of trash I've seen in a long time and you know how easy it is to find trash. Knock this stuff off; it isn't the least bit funny.
—Kathryn, saferinternet.com

this is disgusting and completely wrong. How could you blaspheme Our Lord and Saviour in this horrible way, are you not afraid of the consequences? You really should re-think your position on this.
—Patricia, yahoo.com

BARF!!!!!!!!!
—unsigned, springnet1.com

You have got to be kidding !!!!!!!!!!
He is not a saint,,,,,,,,,,,,, He's the Devil !!!!!!!!!!!!!
—unsigned, sbcglobal.net

This is gross!! I see nothing funny about this. It is done in poor taste.
—Regina, aol.com

you are a disgrace
—unsigned, aol.com

Your creation is truly tasteless. To make money by defacing a sacred picture of God is despicable. I hope you will see the error in your ways and come back to the Church.
—Erika, hotmail.com

This is so disgusting - - you should not make fun of Jesus this way unless you have no fear or respect of His Father and Him.
—Melody, hotmail.com

Your despicable aim is to profit from anti-Catholic bigotry.
—Herman, bowdoin.edu

This adulteration of an image of Our Lord Jesus Christ is insulting to Christians. If you want to promote Mr. Clinton, then do so emphasizing his policies and successes. DO NOT BLASPHEME GOD BY PORTRAYING HIS SON, JESUS, AS SOMEONE HE IS NOT!
—Thomas; Gramercy, Louisiana

I AM APPALLED AT THIS. YOU SHOULD BE ASHAMED OF YOURSELF. CLINTON IS NO SAINT AND EVEN THO' IT IS SUPPOSE TO BE FUNNY, IT IS NOT. GOD FORGIVE YOU!!!!!!!!!!!!!
—unsigned, camtel.net

Irresponsible people resort to abortion to make their lives more comfortable

I have seen your bibs and the "I love abortion" message they carry. They are an outrage to the innocent child who is wearing them and to the senses of those reading that message. I am wondering if you have any children. How sad that you would use an innocent child to deliver such a controversial message. Anyone who has had a little baby and has experienced the love generated by the wonder of childbirth would be horrified by seeing that message.

Unfortunately, sexual relations are treated casually today and irresponsible people resort to abortion to make their lives more comfortable. The child is definitely the victim. You are adding to this situation by using the child to deliver a message that is against the natural law.

If you were to die today, how would you defend your actions to God, the creator of life? I pray your heart will change.

—Loretta, bellsouth.net

Christians are just going to preach to you, which is the last thing you want

Hey, I think you're really talented, Scott, and I find your stuff really amusing, especially when you refer to it as your "art." That's rich, indeed.

I think you're wasting your time, though, making sport of Catholic devotion and poking fun at Christians generally. Christians are just going to preach to you, which is the last thing you want--am

I right? If you have a little courage your art can have an enormous social impact and you can crack yourself up even more than you do now.

Just think of the hilarious opportunities for disparaging, disdaining, deploring, and denigrating Islam. The comedic possibilities are endless for ridiculing Mohammed and the Koran or for insulting revered Iranian clerics, for example. I bet a gifted artist like you could come up with some really funny stuff.

As I say, you've got to have some balls if you're going to flip people off while telling them you mean no offense. Invite some incensed Islamic fundamentalists to a T-shirt signing of your new "Ayatollahs in Drag" line of merchandise. Christians just aren't going to give you the notoriety you deserve. If you play your cards right, you can be a household name, like Salmon Rushdie. You want to get your head on the 5 o'clock news on Al Jazeera TV, don't you?

But you won't follow this advice, I know, because you're not into it for the bucks, the fame, or the fanatical following obsessed with finally catching up with you in the flesh. You are too much the artist and too ethical, of high moral fiber, a man who loves all God's creatures--a vegetarian, no less, these thirteen years.

Don't let the naysayers get you down. All great artists are misunderstood so you shouldn't be surprised that some folks just don't get it. I mean, it's not like you don't think highly of Christians, after all. You went to Catholic school for twelve long years and you never eat meat on Friday.

Some people just have no sense of humor.

Best regards,
–Dave, rushmore.com

Mormons, Jehovah's Witnesses and terrorists

Dear Scott:

In your response to Brian, under the tittle of "God Says.. He Put the Animals Here for Our Use," you stated that Christians are the only group you know of that try to force their beliefs on others. What about the Mormons and Jehovah Witnesses, that show up at the door? Or the terrorist that belief that if we do not belief the way they do we deserve death? Why not point out all groups instead of just attacking one?

—Cindy, aol.com

Saint Reagan and Saint Bush

After reading the overwhelmingly negative feedback concerning your product, I am left wondering if, had you chosen Ronald Reagan or a George Bush as the model for your image, all those same pious folks would be as offended. Probably wouldn't have gotten much feedback at all, would be my guess. Idiots would probably think it was cute.

So, how can I score a lunchbox? They don't seem to be available, hmm?

—Mark, spinn.net

Nice

Get Fucked
—Dave & Debra, pacbell.net

Doesn't anybody else get the irony here?

I'm a conservative & I'm a Christian. And I think this is the funniest thing I've seen all year.

Doesn't anybody else get the irony here?

Thanks for the laugh!
–Tim, adelphia.net

God says...

I read your responses about Christians and while your artwork is irrelevant to me, your uneducated views on Christianity are sad. Like most people who choose to hate another yours is based on ignorance. To simply take pieces of verses out of the bible and quote those saying this is how Christians should live is absurd at the least. To fully understand the bible you must have a relationship God and communicate with him. So you went to catholic school, that doesn't mean you understand anything. The bible itself is not the key to understanding, God is. One last comment, you say you love all of God's creatures and that is why you are vegetarian. God says in Genesis that he put the animals here for our use. Anyway, I saw no sense in bashing you and I use the term "uneducated" only to describe your view on the subject at hand, not you as a whole.

So, I will say a prayer for you that you may seek God and experience all of the blessings he has in store for you. This is Jesus' love for me that I will pass on to you.

Sincerely,
–Brian, flexitallic.com

Gross irreverence

What BLASPHEMY!! For someone to distort the holy picture depicting the Sacred Heart with the superimposed head of Bill Clinton borders on sacrilege, which is a gross irreverence toward a hallowed person, place, or image. Piece of crap.

—Sam, aol.com

Hello Sam,

I understand that Bill Clinton is a hallowed person, and I apologize if my associating him with Jesus Christ is irreverent to the former president.
It is blasphemy to me that you have no respect for other people's beliefs and artistic expressions if they differ from or are contrary to your own. Millions of people do not believe in Christ and are just as offended by our government's morality-driven policies in what we are told is a country that stands for religious and personal freedoms, with a separation of church and state.

People, places and images are hallowed only by those who believe they hold such a significance. Judge not, lest ye be judged.

- Scott Ritcher

"I'm a Evangelical"

What a stupid joke. Bill Clinton is not a saint!!

Far from it. I'm a Evangelical and I really find this stupid. I'm sure my Roman Catholic Friends are really offended with your art.

—unsigned, charter.net

Bill Clinton quote:

"I firmly believed we should not march into Baghdad ...To occupy Iraq would instantly shatter our coalition, turning the whole Arab world against us and make a broken tyrant, into a latter-day Arab hero ... assigning young soldiers to a fruitless hunt for a securely entrenched dictator and condemning them to fight in what would be an unwinnable urban guerrilla war." [1]

Saddam Hussein quotes:

"Today's friend is tomorrow's adversary." [2]

"I feel ... millions of [people] I'm never going to meet ... say my name to the Almighty every day and ask him to help me." [3]

"I could not be [in power] if I did not believe in a divine plan that supercedes all human plans." [4]

"I believe God wants me to be [in power]." [5]

"Government should welcome the active involvement of people who are following a religious imperative..." [6]

"[They] built [huge houses] while letting schools decay... [they] built up armies and weapons while allowing the nation's infrastructure to crumble..." [7]

George W Bush quotes:

"If the attacks of September 11 cost the lives of 3,000 civilians, how much will the size of losses be in 50 states within 100 cities if it were attacked in the same way in which New York and Washington were? What would happen if hundreds of planes attacked American cities?"[8]

"We will pursue them until they lose their nerves... Now that they have indulged in their evil and crimes, they will suffer a defeat." [9]

"We will chase [them] to every corner at all times. No high tower of steel will protect them against the fire of truth." [10]

FIG. 8

THE BILL CLINTON QUOTE IS ACTUALLY A GEORGE BUSH SR QUOTE, THE GEORGE W BUSH QUOTES ARE ACTUALLY SADDAM HUSSEIN QUOTES, AND THE SADDAM HUSSEIN QUOTES ARE ACTUALLY GEORGE W BUSH QUOTES.

1: CBS News, http://www.cbsnews.com/stories/2003/10/31/60minutes/rooney/main581171.shtml
2: Salon, http://archive.salon.com/books/feature/1999/11/23/bush/index1.html
3: Buzzflash, http://www.buzzflash.com/editorial/03/03/12.html
4: Village Voice, http://www.villagevoice.com/issues/0332/mondo1.php
5: Reporter Interactive, http://www.reporterinteractive.org/news/022603/Bush.htm
6: Arky.org, http://www.arky.org/newaltr/news/gwbushte.htm
7: Fox News, http://www.foxnews.com/story/0,2933,98060,00.html
8, 10: DefendAmerica.mil, http://www.defendamerica.mil/articles/oct2002/a101802a.html
9: BBC News, http://news.bbc.co.uk/1/hi/world/middle_east/2867235.stm

I'm still laughing

Awesome!

I just went through your Saint Clinton page, feedback for said page, and wandered through your store. I'm still laughing. I have to say, however, in rebuttal to some of the other feedback...

I'm Catholic. I like to think that I live my life in a Christian manner. Some of that feedback was anything but Christian and yet it came from people who call themselves such. God has a sense of humor and he built us with one too. To refuse to see the absurdity in a situation is to refuse to look at the situation honestly. Now, how can one live like that?

Whatever.
You Rock.
Regards,
—Tammie, portentinteractive.com

Blind partisan stupidity

Dear Scott Ritcher,

I find it vaguely amusing that you would deface a several hundred year old depiction of one who bore the title of "Prince of Peace" with a late 20th century mass-murderer, adulterer, liar, coveter, blasphemer, and violator of every other one of the Ten Commandments, and most any other sane moral philosophy out there.

More comical, really. I mean afterall, how else could anyone explain away your apparent animosity towards the current mass-murderer-in-chief, but by blind partisan stupidity. Which is damn funny! How many of Clinton's policies does Dubya have to continue and expand for you to adore the guy? You know he has to appeal to his Kentucky "base" too, right? ("Stem cells are bad, mmmkay!")

Oh, right, I forgot the business cycle was probably some sort of Republican/conservative conspiracy. Those guys are always so busy figuring out conspiracies, that I guess they'd need to lend their expertise to engage in a few every so often. So I guess it would be Shrub's fault afterall. Yep, it must be a great right wing conspiracy to cause the business cycle! Damn that Dubya, Hail Emperor Willy!

Lovingly Yours,
—Paul, hotmail.com

ONE LINERS:

Disgusting, insulting, generation of vipers are here.
—A.M.; Houston, Texas

What an insult to all Catholics - Please dump it
—Francis, ellislms.fsnet.co.uk

Those pictures are disgusting and pathetic.
—Tim, yahoo.com

Ho hum. Religion and Humor are so mutually exclusive.....
—Catrin, lonestarhealth.com

Love It! Thanks for all the hard work I know you had to put into this.
—Tom & Deb, comcast.net

Open season on Catholics and Our Lord Jesus Christ

Hi,

As you probably know, your gallery is being protested by the tfp.org (here is a link)

http://www.tfp.org/what_we_do/index/saint_clinton_protest.htm

We experienced a similar e-mail deluge a few years ago, and since I have been sending notes so you can locate where the stuff is coming from; and also know you are not alone! Freedom of expression continues!

Best of luck!
—Laura; Santa Fe, New Mexico

Thank you, Laura. Note to readers: The writer of the above letter is an art museum curator. TFP.org is the web site of The American Society for the Defense of Tradition, Family and Property. "Saint Clinton" was listed on the front page of the site as an "Urgent Action Item" with the headline, "Protest the blasphemous 'Saint Clinton' merchandise."

The accompanying article read, in part: "When graphic designer Scott Ritcher was recently asked why he had made a blasphemous representation of the Sacred Heart with the face of former President Bill Clinton, he responded: 'It was just one of those creative moments where you're just like: Oh wouldn't this be funny?'

"However, his attempt at humor has raised the ire of Catholics who see the depiction as an insult to the Faith and the Sacred Person of Our Lord Jesus Christ. 'To depict anyone, even a saint, as Christ would be insulting,' said TFP Web Editor John Horvat. 'But when the person being depicted as our Savoir is a well-known supporter of abortion, the insult runs much deeper.' Many Catholics see this as the latest episode in a growing trend to denigrate the Faith. 'I read about this stuff every day,' said America Needs Fatima director Robert Ritchie. 'It is almost like someone has declared an open season on Catholics and Our Lord Jesus Christ.'

"...the TFP web site is launching an email campaign to legally and peacefully request that (the distributor) stop selling 'Saint Bill Clinton' merchandise and publish a written apology on their web site. 'Standing together as Catholics, we can take a stand and send this cheap insult to our Faith back where it belongs, in the garbage,' said Mr. Horvat. 'I hope to activate our entire email list to send a big message to Scott Ritcher. I want to let him know that this is not funny and that the open-season on Catholics and Our Lord Jesus Christ is officially closed.'"

With clowns like you

With the likes of you doing this sort of garbage production, no wonder America is going down the drain. Muslims are perfectly entitled to believe that your culture is garbage, your ex-president is garbage, you are garbage. Your production provides sufficient elements for everyone to concur with this view.

With clowns like you, who needs to pay to go to the circus? Only a sick mind could produce such piece of garbage.

Go ahead, have your fun, break down what is left of decency in your country. Become the laughing-stock of America's enemies. Wreck what September 11 left standing.

—Raymond; Perth, Western Australia

Jesus' General

I'm going to write about Saint Clinton on my satirical blog, Jesus' General. The post will include a link to your site. I'd like to also post your postcard image. May I have your permission to do so?

The link should drive some buyers your way. I have over 4000 daily readers. I usually get quite a few sales when I write a post about one of my own Cafe Press items.

Here's a link to Jesus' General. http://patriotboy.blogspot.com
I love Saint Clinton. I wish I had done it.

—Gen. J.C., charter.net

I think I know what you're trying to say, but...

YOU PEOPLE ARE SO FULL OF HATE FOR THE
CATHOLICS, THAT YOU DO NOT STOP TO DESECRATE
OUR BLESSED IMAGES. WHY DON'T YOU TRY TO DO
THAT WITH ANY OTHER RELIGION AND SEE WHAT
KIND OF RESULTS AND PROTESTS AND WHAT OTHER
PROBLEMS IT SHOULD BRING YOU?

WHY DON'T YOU STOP PLAYING WITH CATHOLICS
STATUES AND LOOK SOMEPLACE ELSE FOR YOUR
SICKENING GAMES AND ADVERTISINGS?

YOU MAKE ME SICK.
—unsigned, aol.com

Saturated in Christian propaganda day in and day out

I love it. I also love what you wrote about christians being non-
christian. They don't care that people like me are saturated in
christian propoganda day in and day out. I for one and deeply
offended that our president tries to bring religion into all aspects
of his Administration. Church and state were supposed to be
seperated years ago. He needs to get with the times.

—Odis, yahoo.com

You had me at "It's okay to screw around on your wife"

you're sick you're like the Israelites when they just gained their freedom from Egypt and all their struggles there, at the first sign of trouble they wanted to go back to Egypt and their bondage, because all they could remember was the wonderful food they ate, not all the bad stuff.

Kinda like having more than one child....... you're body sends endorphins into the blood stream to make you forget the pain of childbirth so you're silly enough to do it again!

Clinton was an immoral man, he also shut down military bases, weakening our strength, and basicly sent the message that it's okay to screw around on your wife. Men get kicked out of the military for that, and he was our commander in chief....... what has this country come to anyway?

—unsigned, aol.com

Hysterical reactions of the outraged "Christians"

You rock! I love this image. It is absolutely hilarious to read all the pompous and hysterical reactions of the outraged "Christians." And the picture itself is at least as good as most of the religious icons I've ever seen.

—Chris, comcast.net

Preesh

We are praying for you.
—Kathleen, charter.net

Call me anytime

Dear Scott,

I am writing this letter to express my feelings on your I love abortion merchandise. I am appalled at the notion that you would create merchandise for babies with this slogan on them! Tell me, how are sales? To take this issue and create this merchandise period is beyond me! Tell me Scott, have you ever had an abortion? Did your mother? Have you ever made the choice to abort one of your offspring? Have you ever talked to a woman who has? Are you even aware of the risks involved with the procedure? And in your magazine, have you ever interviewed someone who has worked with women who are contemplating or have had an abortion? How about one of the many post abortive women who are suffering physically or emotionally as a result of the "so-called safe simple" procedure? Or is this just your sick way of making a buck?

You see Scott, I have worked with crisis pregnancies for over 9 years. I have seen the devastion that abortion can bring to individuals and families. There is no humor in this, it is not a joke. I have been fighting the fight and will continue to do so. It is an issue that I donnot take lightly. It is a matter of truth, family preservation, and responsibility for me and most of those in this movement. For those of you that support the abortion industry...it is about money. Quite frankly Scott, I hope you make NONE!

And by the way, if you your magazine wants a quote from me, call me anytime [PHONE NUMBER].

Most Sincerely,
—Dee, net-change.com

I'm making more money now than ever

I have enough money to eat at nice restaurants, wash my car and take the day off work. I own a small business and now I get to keep more of my profits thanks to the Bush tax cuts. I've also given my 6 employees raises the past 3 years. Under Clinton, I made less. When Clinton and Reno attacked Microsoft, my stock dropped and I lost money. But I've recovered that and more. I'm making more money now than ever have and so are my employees.

Your picture is funny though way off base.
–Brent; Louisville, Kentucky

In serious need of psychoanalysis help

I think that you are a sick person. Anyone that can, knowingly, offend all persons of a religious belief by mocking one of the most sacred icons is in serious need of psychoanalysis help. I hope that you will seek the help that you most certainly need.

May God bless you and help your tortured soul.
–Liam, netscape.net

I will do my best to spread negative reports

Yo Whom It May Concern:
I am appalled, disgusted and highly offended by the depiction of clinton as Jesus Christ. It almost makes me feel like retching. I will do my best to spread negative reports in regards to this situation.

–Dawn, bigsky.net

If I am Bill Clinton...

I guess the artist is so desperate... no creativity... no sense of art. Even my 2 year old niece can do this type of art by cut & paste. I'll be so stupid to spend money on any of these items. Anyway, I guess anybody who desperately need attention will do anything just to get it... bad taste, no taste.

Good luck.. anybody who buys this stuff is a sucker and a loser. If I am Bill Clinton, which I am glad I am not, I will even sue the artist.

—Sam, sympatico.ca

Perhaps you were molested by a priest, we all know they're a bunch of perverts (or) Been there, brother

Dear Mr. Ritcher,

I hope you will read this with an open mind, and not succumb to the temptation to delete it. As a former lapsed Catholic and graduate of 13 years of formal Catholic education, I once was where you now find yourself. So perhaps it would be less than Christian of me to criticize your products or behavior. I hated the Church, as you do, and wanted to "stick it" to the God-Man. Perhaps you were molested by a priest (we all know they're a bunch of perverts, right?). Or maybe Sister Mary What's-Her-Name hit your knuckles with a ruler. I'm saying, face what it is that you hate: you hate God, and anyone who believes in Him. This much is clear.

You frame it as a Constitutional argument, but perhaps you might want to study the Constitution in depth someday, as well as learn a little about the foundation of this country. Even Catholic education will not do that for you. You have to be interested enough to inform yourself. There is no "separation of church and state" in the Constitution. That phrase came from a letter of Thomas Jefferson to the Danbury, CT, Baptist Association, in response to their concerns that there could evolve a State Religion, as in England, where everyone must belong. I am sorry to say that that fear has been realized, as the religion of Secular Humanism is now the official state-sanctioned religion in our country. You might consider becoming outraged at that, too.

I don't know everything there is to know about law, but I know one thing: every right you have as an American and a human being, including the right to insult and blaspheme Jesus Christ, comes from God. This is the foundation of all our laws, like it or not. Do you think the UN recognizes your God-given rights? They recognize rights as given by the state or the UN. Such recognition can be withdrawn at any time. Do you think the liberals in this country want to protect your rights? They welcome the secularization of our society, including the abridging of your rights, as soon as you are no longer a "useful idiot" (pardon the expression, but I didn't make it up. It is what Stalinists call those in the West who cooperate in their own destruction at the hands of socialism).

God doesn't force, he persuades. But sometimes people who feel convicted about their lifestyle or behaviors become angry when things of God are discussed. I know I did. You are probably fuming right now, and I believe I have been gentle and charitable with you. That's why you hate to even listen to these televangelists. Been there, brother.

Do not think I am anti-free enterprise. That's not it at all. Do not think that I am trying to persecute you and others who are anti-Christian. I am simply trying to explain that the founders of this country were godly men, and the system they set in place can only work for a godly people. Any other type of people cannot remain free, as the nation will eventually sink into anarchy, chaos and finally dictatorship. You make the point that so much of our domestic and foreign policy is made from a Christian standpoint. If our country was founded on these principles, is it a surprise that we should be living them? I think your real point is that you hate Bush, too. Well, he's not my first choice for 2004 either, but not for the same reasons. My reasons are that he spends too much, and is not pro-life enough, is not protecting the borders and is not doing anything substantial to support marriage as an institution created by God. He is also allowing UN monitors in to monitor OUR elections, as if these dictatorial scoundrels need to keep their eyes on US! I am sure your reasons are quite different, and that our political views couldn't be more divergent.

This will probably annoy you, as it may sound condescending, but I will truly pray for you. By the way, your artwork is very good quality, and the Clinton head on the body of Jesus is seamless. I hope you can find ways to be successful by using other topics less controversial.

Sincerely,
–Christopher; Fairburn, Georgia

Ich weiß, aber danke

This is extremly primitiv what I see on your special exhibition o "Saint Clinton".

with best regards

–Hermann; Bad Säckingen, Germany

You obviously are not a true believer

BLASPHEMY!!!!! Don't worry about my opinion, but God will judge any comparing of Clinton (or anyone else) to Jesus Christ. You obviously are not a true believer, otherwise such BLASPHEMY would never have entered your mind or manifested into cups & mugs! God help your soul!

(a true believer)
—Kevin, johndeere.com

Kevin, To people who don't believe what you do, blasphemy doesn't exist any more than the Tooth Fairy, leprechauns, unicorns or Chewbacca. - Scott Ritcher

It is hardly a laughing matter

Dear Mr. Richter,

Your "I Love Abortion" merchandise is offensive. 42 million babies have been slaughtered since Roe v. Wade. What do you think when you hear that number? What do you think of when you think about abortion? Do you know the suffering of the babies and their mothers and fathers? It is hardly a laughing matter.

—Leigh; Altoona, Pennsylvania

Your idiocy is going to hurt Kerry

Are you a Republican plant, or just stupid?!

Your "art" is pissing off many Catholics, who usually vote Dem.

This is a tough race and your idiocy is going to hurt Kerry. Read the blogs, between your Clinton crap, and the "I love abortion", you are getting more of the Christian right angry.

If President Bush is re-elected, you have your own sorry ass to help blame!!

—Michael, verizon.net

Totally gross

Dear Sir:
Your bright idea to advertise abortion is totally gross and wrong. I hope you will rethink your decision, and remove any such articles from the market. We're praying for you.

Sincerely,
—Norbert & Marlene, aol.com

Someone might think those items would be great

Dear Scott,

I am upset, that even as a joke, you would make "I love abortion" baby bibs, etc. Our country is so sick, and someone might think those items would be great. Please, do not continue with this sick joke.

Sincerely,
—Stella; Huntsville, Texas

Congratulations

A few years ago I did something similar, pasting the head of Richard Nixon over a sacred heart picture that I had found on the street somewhere and pasting photocopies of the result all over DC. This was before the internet was the Big Thing that the kids are all in to these days. In any case, congratulations for creating the furor that I never could.

Yours,
—Kevin, comcast.net

To bark in the offense of all fresh

I know that you glory in this but you are an affront to every Catholic in this and in all countries as if not an affront to all Christians for daring to take the Holy and Sacred Heart of Jesus to bark in the offense of all fresh.

What you have just managed to do is move yourself deeper into an eternity of pain, regret, rembembering of your joy at the time of your sin and your failure to care about it when you had your little joke at the expense of millions. I am certain that there would have been a better way to recieve the prayer you are so in need of...why didn't you simply ask. Even so you can get down on your knees and as for Jesus' forgiveness and ask Him to come into your heart so you can know a saint from the adversary from now on.

I WILL be praying urgently for your sorry soul.

Catholic and Christian
—Victoria, iolinc.net

Latin's not dead!

Your bibs are sick! I pray for your soul.

+JMJ+
—Kelly, comcast.net

"The further you withdraw from earthly things, The closer you approach heavenly things, The more you find God. St John of the Cross"

Ave Maria, gratia plena, Dominus tecum. Benedicta tu in mulieribus, et benedictus fructus ventris tui, Iesus. Sancta Maria, Mater Dei, ora pro nobis peccatoribus, nunc, et in hora mortis nostrae. Amen.

SHORTS:

I love it! It's SO true.
Now, we've got the Anti-Christ in the White House and I hope we can get it the hell out!
—Terry; New Jersey

You are one sick man. I'll pray for you. By the way, I hope you have a lawyer. That Sacred Heart image is copyrighted and you're bound to be sued for this.
—Tim, catholic.org

Losers....
—unsigned, aol.com

you gotta be kidding me
—Mark, tekelec.com

Grow up and obtain a heart

Dear Kcomposite,

I would simply like to say that your company has a sick sense of humor. Your so called humorous baby items displaying the message "I love abortion" are sick and twisted. You might as well be making fun of someone's loss of a loved one or something else just as morbid and heart wrenching. All I have to say is grow up and obtain a heart.

Sincerely,
–Shelly "who will never be your customer," earthlink.net

Yet another letter equating abortion with the Holocaust

Dear Sir,

I just finished reading an article about your "I love abortion" baby bibs. You know what would be funny? If cocky liberals as yourself would aquire a shed of respect for human life in all its stages. Im a 22 year old College student. Ive seen and heard a lot of pro choice people spittin off there rhetoric that it isnt a baby or a life. Nazis said the same thing about Jews and guess what Slave owners said the same thing about Black people. 4000 abortions every year and your cracking jokes. How little you know about the beauty of all human life. since Roe V. Wade 40,000,000 babies in America have been killed. around the world the total is about 500,000,000 little lives snuffed out never having a voice on earth all becuase of the spineless guise called choice. And you crack jokes and dare to turn the worst onslaught on human life in the history of the world into an oppurtunity to make money and appear to funny to your liberal comrades. You may feel proud of yourself because of your achievement but it is nothing to be proud about. You should be ashamed of yourself and unable to look at yourself in the mirror. May God show you the value of all human life.

God Love You,
—Christopher, hotmail.com

I hope so, because I was laying it on pretty thick

Dear Scott:

What a great idea - putting "I Love Abortion" on t-shirts. I worked in marketing for years and I have some more suggestions for you. How about "I Love Suicide" for the pro-euthanasia folks, or "I Love Murder" for those on death row and finally, "I Love Terrorists Who Decapitate People" for Osama bin Laden and his followers? W'dya think?

—Kathleen, msn.com

I love humor!

Scott,

If your reasoning behind the "I Love Abortion" baby bibs is that "Babies, of all people, would never love abortion," so that "takes the joke that much farther," the humor really isn't apparent, Scott, as much as I would like to see it. Hence, why not redo the bib with something that more clearly reflects humor? What might that be? That's where creativity comes in, and I'm sure you could come up with something. But get plenty of opinions as to whether your product truly is humorous.

Be open to the possibility of not finding something humorous regarding abortion, as with other isssues. Would a Jew where an "I Love the Holocaust" t-shirt? You say you will not cross that line. You already did with your products.

Perhaps, in the end, your products will have to state reality, if they can't be humorous about it. How's this for baby bibs: "I survived Abortion," "I survived the womb, the most dangerous place in America" since one in four pregnancies in the United States ends in abortion. There's irony: the womb is the most dangerous place in American--not an inner city barrio (like where I live), not fighting in Iraq (which is much safer than the womb in America, 1% of the troops stationed there have died over the course of more than two years, versus the 43,750 that would have had to die over a two-year period to match abortion mortality in the U.S.)...

No one likes The Three Stooges more than me! I love humor! Your products are not humorous in the least.

—Fausto, juno.com

A poor choice to bring attention to the abortion debate

Scott

Your line of merchandise is a poor choice to bring attention to the abortion debate, granted that the "I had a abortion" T shirts are in incredible poor taste and in fact are indefensible. Please find a better way to promote your magazine and bring attention to the absurdity of abortion. God doesn't want us to kill unborn children, it's a terrible sin to do so.

—Ned, parlorcity.com

You seem to arrogantly know exactly what you are doing

You have done and supported a terrible blasphemous deed. Unlike those who executed Our Lord, you seem to arrogantly know exactly what you are doing. Only grace from the One that you mock can save you from yourselves.

–Nathan, hotmail.com

May you re-think your ethical standards

To Whom This May Concern:

I have seen your "I Love Abortion" merchandise and would have to say that I am appalled. Even though they were produced in a way that was to expose finatical ideas, it makes me sick to my stomach that someone would actually buy it. As long as you promote and sell products such as these I will never support and encourage others not to support your magazine. May you re-think your ethical standards.

-Mark, bellarmine.edu

p.s. I am President of Bellarmine Students for Life, and if no action is taken, something will be brought up to our group of 70 members about this.

The product of an evil mind

Your "I Love Abortion" items are disgusting and represent the product of an evil mind. Your premise is that you hate life - not a very uplifting point of view.

You say you would never "joke" about the Holocaust or slavery, but abortion is our nation's No. 1 Holocaust having killed over 40 million and still counting unborn children.

Abortion is a poor choice for women and it dooms them to a slave mentality and an unrewarding emotional life in their love relationships. None of which is material for laughs. In the final analysis, you may make a few bucks but it's blood money.

—Mary; Forsyth, Missouri

Many liberals fight for the life of chickens on farms, but immediately support the murder of a child

Mr. Richter,
I am sure that my comments and opinions mean nothing to you, but I felt compelled to respond. What you consider a joke only confirms the decline of our society. Since when is the murder of a child funny? Many Liberals fight for the life of chickens on farms, but immediately support the murder of a child. What kind of a society puts the lives of animals above that of a child simply because it cannot yet speak for itself. Abortion is simply an act of selfishness. Why is it ok to teach our society that you can take the lives of innocent children because they may be a personal burden? I don't believe in the abuse or killing of animals by humans unless used for food or to end pain. However, I also don't believe in killing babies. I am curious as to why you feel the need to support such a view as you did in the article released by LifeNews.com. I am someone who has tried to have children and so far have been unable to do so. My husband and I are looking into adoption. There are so many couples who are willing and wanting to adopt, even those who can bear their own children.

Supporting and encouraging the act of abortion does not really help anyone. In the end it breeds irresponsibility and desensitization to murder in all senses. Does it really help a young couple to encourage such an act without thoroughly explaining to them what the repercussions may be (Planned Parenthood)? They may have horrible nightmares for the rest of their life, may suffer from health related issues, may carry with them psychological baggage that could damage the relationship with their future spouse and/or could encourage them to use abortion as a type of birth control. There are so many good reasons not to support abortion and really not any good reasons to support it. It saddens me to watch our nation in such decline. It is ironic, I believe in many issues that Democrats and Liberals believe in, but I also believe in rational not theoretical solutions such as the sanctity of life no matter animal or human, preservation of the environment through conservation and self responsibility rather than ranting and raving about non-realistic solutions, that truth and character matter more than individuality and that "Freedom" is not defined as the absence of morality, rationale, common sense, sacrifice and Christianity. Mr. Richter you will be in my prayers, as will all who support a nation without an absolute truth.

–Tammy, msn.com

I will pass the word on to others

Dear Mr. Richter,

I heard about your "I love abortion" products and looked at them on your website. You were quoted as saying "The bibs, and all the 'I love abortion' items, are designed as a humorous depiction of how far some people take certain issues. Babies, of all people, would never love abortion." I can understand your attempt to make fun of things, but really this is NOT funny. It is in extremely bad taste. I can't imagine what sort of sick customer would buy these products. Would you think a t-shirt saying "I love 9-11" is funny? If so I doubt many other people would.

I hope you are not selling any of these items, but the world being what it is now a days I wouldn't be surprised if you were. I certainly will not have anything to do with a company that sells such items and you can be assured I will pass the word on to others.

—Kari, cableaz.com

I have forwarded your website... to just as many people as I can influence to boycott your website

I am absolutely heartsick that you would find a market for such offensive products.

I have forwarded your website to everyone in my address book as well as to just as many people as I can influence to boycott your website.

You should be ashamed.

—Catherine, aol.com

Medical doctor, specializing in creative punctuation

Dear Friend,

You should read this pro-life news article from LifeNews.com: http://www.lifenews.com/nat815.html

Dear Scott, Have you ever wondered what you will say when you face your Lord, who made you, at the last day? Perhaps about the \""I Love Abortion\" merchandise? I believe in this life there is a battle between the Lord and the devil for our eternal souls and I, for one, wish to be on the Lord\'s side. Your merchandise is not. He tells us, \"Thou shall not kill\", even in gest. I shall pray for you.

Best Wishes,
—Paula, M.D., provide.net

QUICK BITS:

THIS IS A JOKE RIGHT? NOBODY IN THEIR RIGHT MIND WOULD THINK OF THIS JOKE OF A PRESIDENT AS A SAINT!!!!!!!!!!!
—Elva, comcast.net

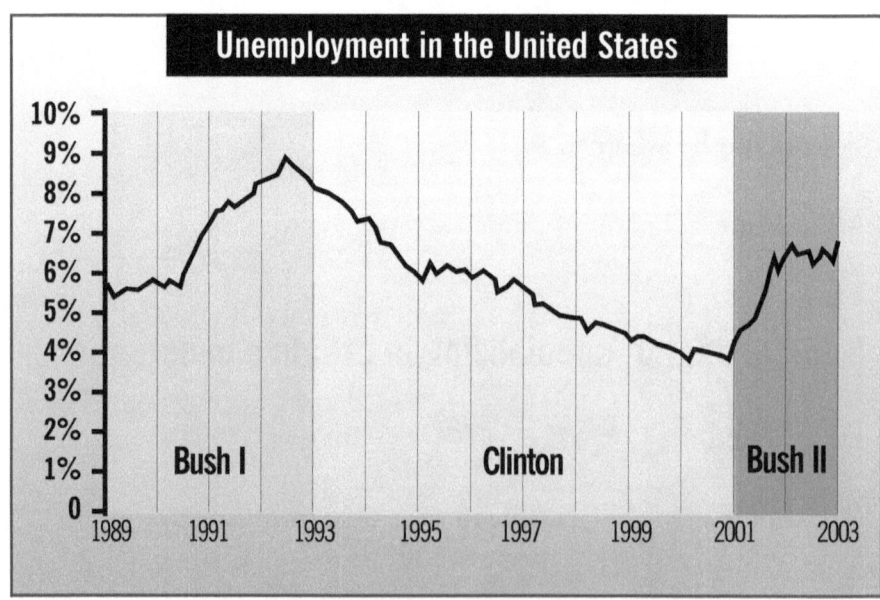

Fig. 9: Unemployment in the U.S. since 1989

"I LOVE ABORTION"??? DON'T BE SUCH AN IDIOT!
—G.E., furryllama.com

Hi,
Since you now have I Love Abortion tee shirts, could you maybe
do some "I love genocide" or "I love concentration camps" or "I
love Hitler" or "I love murder" tee shirts.
Thanks.
—Paul, iol.ie

Get a life!
—Karen , earethlink.net

"But what happens to the baby?"

Dear Scott,

You love abortion? Then you never had a family member whose
entire life was changed because of it. You have never lived with
their suffering and pain.

You love abortion? Then you have never tried to explain it
"objectively" to your seven-year-old daughter, who heard the
word on the school bus. You have not heard her question, "But
what happens to the baby?" then not had an answer. You have
not heard her sobs when she said, "The baby dies!"

You love abortion? Then you do not realize the victimization
women who undergo abortion often feel. For many, it is not a
choice. It is a result of pressure from the people they love most.
It is a lack of choice in a desperate time.

You love abortion? Then you have never felt the soft, sweet skin
of a baby, your own child, and known that this tiny person is

more precious to you than your own life. You don't know the love of a mother for her little one, a love that overwhelms you for a lifetime.

You love abortion? Why do you not, instead, love life?

Sincerely,
–Johnny, misn.com

Zephaniah 3:17 The LORD your God is with you, he is mighty to save. He will take great delight in you, he will quiet you with his love, he will rejoice over you with singing.

Women do have freedom of choice – even in the case of rape – freedom to choose to give the child up for adoption

Mr. Richter,

There can never be anything humorous about abortion. It is a horrendous act of murder against a completely innocent and defenseless human being and a violent attack on women as well. The latest technology in ultrasound imaging shows beyond any doubt that these are little human persons being killed inside their mothers' wombs. Even w/o such technology, simple logic informs the simplest of minds that a meaningless blob of tissue does not grow into a human being - nor do women carry insects or animals in their wombs who suddenly become humans upon birth. It is madness to think that the united sperm and ovum, then embryo and then fetus inside a woman's uterus are anything but the first stages human development as are the child, the teen, the middle-aged person and the senior. Some may say that at these earliest stages the human person does not look like a human being and therefore must not be. That is immature and ignorant. A victim of severe burns or physical trauma often ceases to look human, but no one in their right mind would say that they no longer are. It is no less illogical to say that because the human person before 23 weeks or so is not able to survive outside the womb they are thus not human. Is a baby, once born, not human since he/she cannot survive without the complete assistance of another human being? No. Is a person who falls off a horse a human one day, but no longer a human now that he is suddenly paraplegic and totally dependent upon others? Any person who would answer yes to this question is applying the fascist philosophy of Hitler, the Nazis, Margaret Sanger, the KKK, etc. This philosophy rates the sick, the elderly - anyone deemed not highly productive to the "machine" - inhuman and marked for "removal". It is Hitlerism philosophy to deem the unborn whose conception was not planned or who are handicapped subhuman and marked for removal since their life is thought to cause inconvenience.

You said you would never joke about the Holocaust or slavery. Mr. Richter, please I beg you, open your eyes! Think a little bit! Margaret Sanger, the founder of Planned Parenthood, was a great admirer of Adolph Hitler. Her goal was eugenics - ethnic cleansing - same goal as Hitler! This is not something I'm making up - you can read it for yourself in her own documents! Her mad plan was to cleanse the world of the non-whites by targeting the ethnic communities and third world countries with contraception, sterilization and abortion - it was never about caring for women or their "freedom of choice". Again, you can read all this in her own public words! We women DO have freedom of choice - the freedom to choose to be responsible or not with the great gift entrusted to us of bringing children into this world - even in the case of rape (pregnancy as a result is rare), we women have the freedom to choose to give that innocent child up for adoption rather than punishing him/her for his/her father's crime by killing him/her. The Jewish people and other victims of the holocaust were deemed subhuman by Hitler, the slaves were deemed subhuman by their masters and much of society, and now the pre-born who are unplanned for or handicapped are deemed subhuman. Have you ever studied how they are killed? The suffering of the victims of the holocaust and that of the slaves was horrendous to say the least, but the suffering endured by the preborn killed by abortion is infinitely worse: they have absolutely no possible means of escape or self-defense; they are either cut to pieces and vacuumed out, burned from the inside out with saline solution, removed and suffocated or left to die, or their brains are sucked out. This is worse than Hitler. This is worse than whipping and lynching - this is unimaginable evil and it is happening every minute of every day in this country - the USA - and it is legal.

This is NOTHING TO BE JOKING ABOUT!

As a magazine editor, you have the potential to reach hundreds of people and help stop this. Don't be like the Germans who did nothing or who rationalized that the Jews were subhuman anyway; don't be like the racists of yesterday and today. Don't choose to think illogically and incompletely just because that serves the modern god of convenience. It was Hitler and the other fascist industrialists who propagandized efficiency and convenience as the highest virtues to be sought after at the expense of all persons, things or ideas which get in the way.

Your magazine interviews common folks. I challenge you to interview women who have had abortions, men whose girlfriends/wives have aborted their children w/o telling them first; grandparents whose grandchildren have been aborted because parental consent is not required for minors - and I challenge you to do this in an HONEST unbiased manner.

Or, are you no better than the slave owners, Hitler or the people who turned a blind eye to these victims?

—Margarita, sgintl.com

Must stay cool. Stay cool. Stay cool. I CAN'T DO IT!

Scott, I feel very sorry for you. Apparently, you do not believe God exists or that you have an eternal soul that will live FOREVER. That word FOREVER, alone, is almost beyond my imagination! You do not die, Soctt, when you leave this life. You will then pay for your transgressions on this earth. We do get payback, if not in this life, in the next - believe me. What goes round; does come around.

I will pray that you will see how horrible what you are doing by selling these "I love abortion shirts" is. You may get rich, you may not feel bad, you may even get praise from some people; however, WHAT YOU ARE DOING IS BEYOND SLAVERY OR THE HORROR OF PERSECUTION OF MANY OF THE PEOPLE WHO WERE PERSECUTED IN THE PAST AGES OR PRESENT. YOU ARE MOCKING THE LIVES OF MILLIONS OF LITTLE INNOCENTS IN THE WOMB WHO ARE BEING SLAUGHTERED EVERY SECOND OF EVERY DAY.

—unsigned, aol.com

Bo-o-o-o-oring!

may God have mercy on you, he is the only one who will, you media seeking snake....
—unsigned, comcast.net

We always need some good, clever, even in-your-face pro-life merchandise

Dear Scott,

I think you may have meant to spoof Planned Parenthood recent outrageous "I had an abortion" t-shirt with your "I Love Abortion" merchandise. However, abortion is just one subject that has no humor in it - how could the painful slaughter of millions of babies?

You might want to check http://www.michaeljr.org for clarity. This is the soul-wrenching, first-hand account of a young woman who had an abortion this year in Cincinnati.

By the way, we always need some good, clever, even in-your-face pro-life merchandise. But this is not the best approach to take.

regards,
—Paula, cincinnatirighttolife.org

Saint Elvis

St Clinton - Haven't laughed that hard in weeks. And your bumper stickers - I can't decide! ahh!

PLEASE PLEASE PLEASE do a St. Elvis. You'd make a fortune.

My god, I'd have to have one of those too.

—Jen, verybigdesign.com

Thank you for breaking the silence

Scott, thank you for breaking the silence around this issue. Any time we can get people to talk about abortion, we have an opportunity to point out what it really is. That is good. The lies around abortion are pretty thick, however. We have a California legislator, Maxine Waters, who marched in support of abortion last January in D. C. She carried a sign which said, "I'm for Choice, because my mother didn't have one" ????!!!!!

Thanks again for speaking up. Tell the truth and shame the devil!

–Christine, cal.net

I thought there were decent people in Kentucky

You must be a complete and total IDIOT to depict as a saint a man who has done everything in his power to destroy the USA! That man is about as far from being a saint as anyone could be. I hope that arrogant asshole sues you for using his image.

A baby bib that pro-death baby bib!!! What kind of a SICKO PERVERT are you, anyway!?!?!???? I thought there were decent people in Kentucky but you have certainly changed my mind about that! You need to have your head examined.

Apparently you do not care who you offend with your trash. You and the trash you produce are an affront to decent people everywhere Your face should be painted on the ass-end of a horse!!!

–Ron, connections-etc.net

Regardless of it being Clinton or not

Sir,

I just wanted to express that I found your image of President Clinton as Christ to be very offensive. You said that you were not intending to offend people. Well, you have indeed done so. Any truly believing Christian should consider this to be an offensive image, which I'm sure you can understand if you think about it from our perspective. This is regardless of it being Clinton or not. I don't believe anyone should be portrayed as Christ except for Christ Himself. Surely, as well, it would be inappropriate were it some other religion's holy figure. No one enjoys having the object of such deep beliefs mocked in such a way. I ask that you would reconsider what you are doing here.

–Brian, yahoo.com

You're either with us, or you're with the terrorists (or) Priests for Life: (insert your own joke here)

There is nothing funny about abortion or anything (intended joke or otherwise) that appears to support it. There is no middle ground on this issue, you are either pro-abortion or you are pro-life. Those that claim to be undecided are pro-abortion as well since they do nothing to try and stop it.

I urge you to go out to http://www.priestsforlife.org/resources/photosassorted/index.htm and look at their gallery of aborted babies and see if you still find your "joke" amusing.

–Carolyn, zion.gotmc.net

As we know, no one really loves abortion

I just read about the news in your so called magazine about selling items on-line promoting pro-abortion items such as baby bibs etc-saying things like I Hate Abortion-this is disgusting and repulsive-I was bad enough that Planned Parenthood had the t-shirts that said I had an Abortion-now this-they have really gone too far this time-and are pushing it more-as we know no one really loves abortion-as such it is just a way that Planned Parenthood has for taking care of a problem-a baby-they say that is not a human life at all-it is a inconveinence-get rid of it like trash that it is-the abortion will solve everything-but make no mistake about it-it is not the end-they just think so-it is only the beginning of a life filled with sorrow,despair,guilt and it will and does effect you for the rest of your life whether they want to beleive it or not-so this latest promotion is extremely crude and just shows how ignorant Planned Parenthood is in all of this area.They do not want to know the baby is a human being because if they did they would have to admit to murdering babies every single day and that would be too much for their so called perfect world where Babies are killed for the sake of it not being the right time or just an inconveinence in their lives at this time!

—Jackie, aol.com

Help to spread the word about my music and mission

Hi, my name is Ylond Miles-Davis. I read your article and you are doing some interesting art. Will you please visit my web site at www.ylondmilesdavis.com.

I just launched it on Sept 15, 2004 on the Feast day of Our Lady of Sorrows. It would be great if you could add my link on your site. I would appreciate some visitors and help to spread the word about my music and misson.

Sincerely,
–Ylond; Brentwood, California

You have a few issues to resolve

Dear Scott:

I pray that you always have good health and hopefully stay young and be a productive member of society. Because, since we have started killing innocent children we have become a culture of death. It will not be long before they start putting the elderly or the sick to death. We do not wish for them to be a drain on society, now do we?

As far as the picture goes, it shows that you have a few issues to resolve. Christians are not perfect, they are only struggling to be the best they can be and they fall and they fall often. The only perfect person is the Lord who died on the cross for us. He is a merciful God and probably understands your hatred better than you do. There is that age old question, "what if there is no God, then you wasted your life in believing in him"? No, I just lived a life being kind to my fellow brothers and sisters, trying to be the best I could be. For me, life did not become interesting until I got to know the Lord. I had a life full of parties, friends, and money, but was still bored and empty. It was not until the Lord entered the picture that my life got really exciting. That was nineteen years ago and the excitement has not stopped yet.

Hopefully one day you will find fulfillment in this life without finding it necessary to attack other people's beliefs. Thanks to the constitution you have the freedom to offend people and we are asked to be tolerant of your rights. What about extending the same rights to us?

I am sorry you were hurt by people that called themselves Christians. The problem is that men are not God. And again, man is not perfect. Whatever happened to make you so critical of Christians was done by men, who make mistakes and plenty of them. I'm guessing that in you have made a mistake or two during your time on this earth. What did you hope for forgiveness or ridicule? You are comparing apples to oranges when you compare God to man.

God Bless,
–Cindy, aol.com

Can't we leave Hitler out of this?

Mr. Richter, I understand you're bemused by the reactions of Catholics to what we believe to be blasphemy. Well then, if you're in it for the chuckles, may I suggest a few innovative ideas to facilitate the hillarity? Why not make an Adolf Hilter picture and make a few minor changes, like put a yarmulke on his head and substitute the swatzika for a Star of David? Here's another idea – make a picture of Dr. Martin Luther King Jr, but put Ku Klux Klan robes on him. Think those are great ideas? Why or why not? Be honest now, and maybe you'll answer your own questions about the offense that we Catholics take to such crass stupidity.

–Janet, erols.com

LAST ROUND OF SHORTS:

God please help the people who create this kind of garbage that they may see that this is wrong. In Jesus precious name I Pray. Amen. I will not send this to anyone because it would offend everyone I know. Blasphemer's!!
—unsigned, aol.com

Though your attempt was justifiable, you product is not. If a product has to be explained, it's not a good product. Please reconsider selling these items. Thank you.
—Vicki, harenet.net

GREAT! I'd love to see this get MUCH wider exposure than just in emails from friends! Thanks!
—Renee, redshift.com

From what I read on our Pro-Life email you have a sick sense of humor. Please redirect your efforts to something worthwhile. What you have done is disgusting.
—Fran, bellsouth.net

Your "I love abortion" products are HORRIBLE!!!!!!!!!! I am sickened by them and by your site for selling these things.
—Kerry, msn.com

We should have known it would be only a matter of time until the demogogues elevated "their" man to "supreme leader"....Theirs only....the god who "sees nothing as evil....hears no evil concerning himself and does only evil.
—unsigned, aol.com

I find this disgusting and inappropriate. I will pray for you and the artist.
—Stewart, iquest.net

This is a joke, right? Yes or no, it is in extremely poor taste.
–Sheila, aol.com

Scott, I am still praying for you. So are others.
–Greg, earthlink.net

I think this is disgusting & an utter disgrace.
–Denise, aol.com

Very tacky.
–Wendy, aol.com

[blank message]
–Phillip, faa.gov

BILL-IANT!!! I mean, brilliant!!!! I know where I'm doing my
online Xmas shopping this year. All my republican fiends... I
mean, friends, (both of them) will be fuming!
–Tim, mindspring.com

I liked President Clinton a lot and I voted for him twice, but Saint
Clinton is SICK.
–Paul, direcway.com

Love it!!!! Where can I get coasters and a lunchbox? I'll take St.
Clinton over that he-devil in the White House any day.
–Cheryl; Lafayette, California

This scene truly turns my stomach and makes me take notice of
the Biblical prediction of abominations being committed during
the end times! Life is short...Go for it! Push For Bush, Cuz Kerry
IS Scary!
–Jeannie, sbcglobal.net

Are you out of your mind? Or perhaps out of your spirit! What
an insult. Thank you for joining the rest of the cartoon journalists

in their futile assault on Christianity, in particular the Catholic Church. Yes, this website is most assuredly a stain on you soul. May God help you.
—Denny, myfam.com

Apparently, babies have opinions on fashion

Hello, I see that on your website you sell a bib that says "I love abortion."

Since abortion ends a life, what's the point of putting the above phrase on a bib, an item that is usually put on a baby? I don't think any baby would really want to wear such a thing, since they'd probably be happy to be alive.
Thanks for your insight.

—Caroline; Virginia

My point can be best made with a quote from "Hook"

Mr. Ritcher, I didn't see the article regarding St. Clinton until yesterday. I do have to say, you are a talented sketch artist. I'm sorry that you have to demean your talent by drawing a picture of Clinton portrayed as though he, too, were the Sacred Heart of Christ. Not that Jesus doesn't hold Clinton in his heart - as I'm sure he does. However, as they say in "Hook", I think you showed bad form. I'm sorry you have to make fun of Christian beliefs and true saints (many of whom were martyred for their belief in Jesus), just to raise a little debate. You won't be the last to persecute Christians. You are very talented, Mr. Ritchie. Have a good life, and God bless you.

—Sharon, strausstroy.com

There has been only one man in all of history... who was and is perfect

I woke up this morning and said a prayer for you. I too am Catholic, I am human, I also make mistakes. I am not perfect and do not claim to be. To my knowledge there has been only one man in all of history that walked the face of this earth who was and is perfect. He died for you and me... for the sins we have committed against the Father... for our disobedience to His Law. Jesus gives us an example of what it means to be obedient to the Father even unto death. Death on a Cross. He gives us each the opportunity to follow him and receive the eternal reward of heaven. Whichever image you chose of Him, be it of a European or Middle-Eastern makes no difference. Yes, he made us all in His image, even Mr. Clinton. That does not excuse your use of a sacred image as a means to mock and stir up anger in Christians everywhere for your personal amusement.

If you truly have lost touch with the significance of this image, and who Christ was. I suggest you do some serious reflection on it in prayer.

I will continue to ask the Father to have mercy on your soul and speak to your heart.

—Mike, ev1.net

A very confused person who... is asking for help

Quote:"I would urge those who are offended by my art to try to imagine where it may have come from. Look at the country and the world from the other side. And judge not, lest ye be judged."

That's not art. . . That is a cheap blasfemous photo manipulation. Where it may come from? From a very confused person who lost his faith somewhere, sometime on the walk of life and is asking for help, although you may not admit it. . .

God have mercy on you for promoting abortion as "something to laugh about".

I will pray for you so He can illuminate you so you may once again find He who is the Way, the Truth and the Life.

–Gino, yahoo.com

Our Lord will take care of you

I AM DEEPLY OFFENDED BY YOUR SICK HUMOR. I AM SURE EVEN THE CLINTONS ARE OFFENDED AND IF NOT THEN WE ARE REALLY IN TROUBLE IN THIS WORLD. I AM SURE OUR LORD WILL TAKE CARE OF YOU.

–unsigned, aol.com

How dare he

If the artist cannot see the affront in this he is truly in trouble.How dare he mock the Sacred Heart....there is a definite line between humor and sacrilege and he has more than crossed it.....Shame on anyone who puts this trash before the public either on display or for marketing....If he is not a Christian he has still gone too far in offending those who are..

–unsigned, eatel.net

Remember what St. Paul said

I read your comments to the emails from people offended by your St. Clinton piece and wish to add my own two cents.

I think you are missing the point of what so many are saying. While I support your right to create what you wish, I find your criticism of those don't like your piece a little hypocritical.

You seem to be slamming christianity through this piece (yes, I know, you're just poking 'fun.'). If you remember some of your training, however, you should remember the biblical admonition to 'do unto others as you would have others do unto you.' This piece, intentional or not, will be interpreted as blasphemous by many who take their faith seriously. Remember what St. Paul said in his letters, too, that if it would cause his brother to sin, he would never eat meat again? (That of course referred to the dilemma many early followers had about eating meat that was sacrificed to the gods.)

So, by doing this piece of artwork, you are deliberately setting out to offend and hurt others, and cause them to feel their deeply held beliefs are being mocked and ridiculed. Surely you aren't shallow or unimaginative enough to think everyone lives in your universe and would easily follow the 'joke'?

As to your politicizing of christians finding fault with your work (as if that had anything to do with their feelings about the sacred heart of Jesus), that is simply irrelevant. You are dragging other people's beliefs through the mud; what they believe politically doesn't matter.

You are a vegetarian. Fine. I'm not. Does that give me the right to mock your beliefs in my own little art-world creation, and then, if you voice objection, ridicule your complaint by dragging in your political beliefs? And then express disbelief when you just simply don't get the joke?

Show a little consideration for people who think other than you. You can create what you want; no one's stopping you. But at least be honest when you answer their criticism. You're mocking christianity. That's all there is to it; political beliefs: left, right, center, whatever, simply don't enter in. (Except that it seems to be liberal/leftists who seem to do most of the mocking.)

Sincerely,
—Mary; Michigan

Mary, I am constantly ridiculed by others for my vegetarianism, but I understand that not everyone believes what I believe, and so I shrug it off as a difference of opinion. I would never get all bent out of shape or offended by it. I just have to accept that it is just one of my personal beliefs and everyone has their own. ~ Scott

Christ is not to take offense from anything in this world

To whom it concerns, if anyone,
There is really nothing that can be said that would make your "art" or some of the bumper stickers on your site any more ludicrous. The depiction of Clinton as Christ doesn't offend me as the Body of Christ is not to take offense from anything in this world. It is nothing more than a weak attempt at blasphemy by a worldly person who wouldn't know God if He sat beside him. Thus, the painting is powerless.

The bumper stickers referring to Bush as an illegitimate President are indicative of the author's ignorance. They're not offensive by any means, just a representation of willing blindness and hatred. Every single person that has ever served as President of the United States has been elected by the Electoral College, period. Your man lost according to the rules, so you want to change them. Sad.

Go vote for John Kerry, a man who can't even take a stance on an issue and stick with it. Some leader!

—Mike, achaiasolutions.com

He does look quite saintly

My innocent little daughter called me here in Vermont and told me about a scandalous use of the holy card I have been carrying in my wallet for 50 years. I cannot imagine putting that amoral Bill Clinton on the body of Jesus. Actually after looking at it for awhile he does look quite saintly.

I also cannot believe you have caused such a commotion. Some people just don't have a sense of humor. All you need to do now is put Bush's head on Judas' body. Only problem no one would know it was Judas.

Keep the creative juices flowing.

—John, yahoo.com

Your site is great!

Your site is great! Personally I wasn't a big fan of Bill Clinton however I do miss the humor that went along with his Presidency. Definitely a site not to be taken seriously but is "lighthearted".

—Kurt, aecf.org

Superstitious goobers

Scott, you've done it again. Good job on riling up the 14th-century superstitious goobers of Kentucky.

—Jamie, riseup.net

Punctuation champion

have you no shame scott? clinton is a liar and a cheat , and you want to paint him as a saint? . boy your mom didn't teach you right boy, now did she

—Michael, juno.com

Point number one

Hello Scott,
I realize that you might be trying to play a joke with a bib that says I love abortion but there are a few problems with that.

1. Do you realize during the Holocaust German guards at one point called many of the Jewish prisoners to play soccer and act out skits. The guards filmed this to show to the international community that they were treating the Jewish people properly. After the filming all those in the skits/games were killed.

The I love abortion for babies is similar. Babies are being killed in the womb, and we have other babies advertising it. Why would a baby advocate something that could have annihilated herself depending on the mother choice? It doesn't make sense.

Please check out www.cbrinfo.org for better shirts you could sell.

If you recognize this line of clothes is offensive then consider which political candidates support abortion (Bush does not, Kerry does). If it's offensive for a baby to wear this kind of shirt, then why are you promoting a candidate (or bashing Bush) that supports abortion?

Please respond as i really want to hear why you are doing this.

Sincerely,
—Paul, cs.ucf.edu

Back in my day, when we sent somebody a death threat, we at least took the time to spell their name right

My name is Ben [last name] and I am a student at the University of Louisville. I have a new idea for t-shirt slogans. Instead of your FUCKED up "IloveAbortion" baby merchandise, how about this instead:

on the front:
I CHOPPED RICHTER'S BODY UP INTO LITTLE PIECES

then on the back:
AND I LOVED DOING IT

Gee, don't ya think that would just be so hillarious?

You guys are disgusting. Save yourselves the embarrassment, and pull that stuff.

—Ben; Louisville, Kentucky

"My life is great" p.85

Religion-Related Injuries clipping

"With clowns like you" p.142

"Open season on Catholics" p.141

"The reason for 9/11" p.88

American Society for the Defense of Tradition, Family and Property clipping

"It is not too late for you" p.108

"You're going to go and build his ego up" p.58

"Is it worse" p.80

Clinton quote: "If you look back on the Sixties and, on balance, you think there was more good than harm in it, you're probably a Democrat. And if you think there was more harm than good, you're probably a Republican."

"Saint Clinton" digital print on vinyl, 24x36 in.

"Personally, I believe he is a gay" p.128

"You are like the computer genius" p.42

"Sir, I will pray for you" p.86

"Anyone who is angry, doesn't get my sympathy; they should just turn it off." p.47-56, six panels

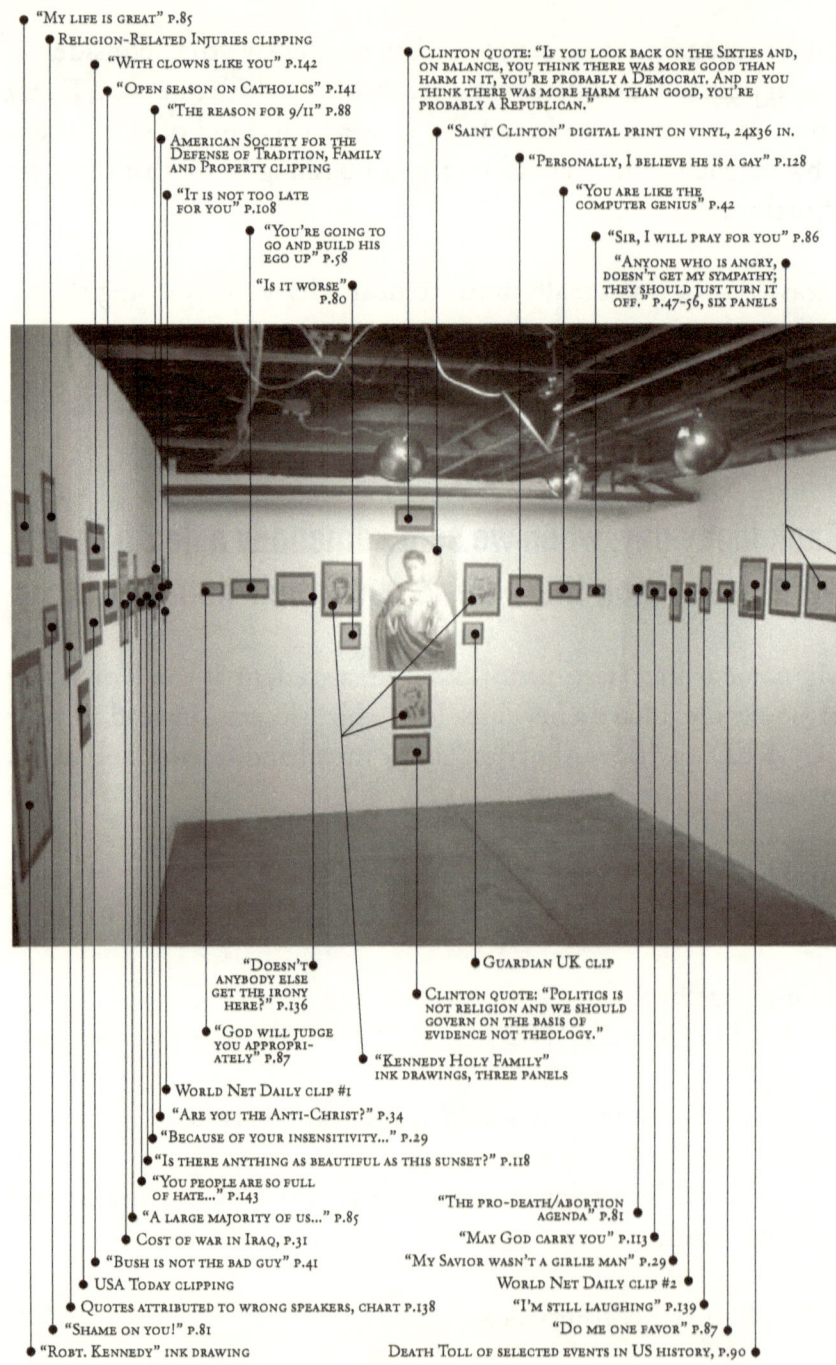

"Doesn't anybody else get the irony here?" p.136

"God will judge you appropriately" p.87

Guardian UK clip

Clinton quote: "Politics is not religion and we should govern on the basis of evidence not theology."

"Kennedy Holy Family" ink drawings, three panels

World Net Daily clip #1

"Are you the Anti-Christ?" p.34

"Because of your insensitivity..." p.29

"Is there anything as beautiful as this sunset?" p.118

"You people are so full of hate..." p.143

"A large majority of us..." p.85

Cost of war in Iraq, p.31

"Bush is not the bad guy" p.41

USA Today clipping

Quotes attributed to wrong speakers, chart p.138

"Shame on you!" p.81

"Robt. Kennedy" ink drawing

"The pro-death/abortion agenda" p.81

"May God carry you" p.113

"My Savior wasn't a girlie man" p.29

World Net Daily clip #2

"I'm still laughing" p.139

"Do me one favor" p.87

Death Toll of selected events in US history, p.90

Fig. 10: Saint Clinton installation
Oct. 1-15, 2004, Swanson Reed Contemporary Gallery, Basement Space, Louisville

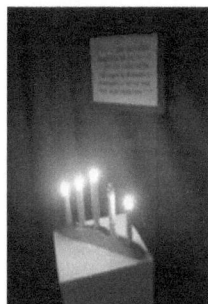

ENTRANCE TO GALLERY:
"ALL OF US HAVE DONE STUPID THINGS IN
OUR LIFE, BUT NONE OF US HAVE HAD
EIGHTY MILLION DOLLARS SPENT BY
THOUSANDS OF INVESTIGATORS TO FIND OUT
WHAT THOSE STUPID THINGS WERE."
—JAMES CARVILLE

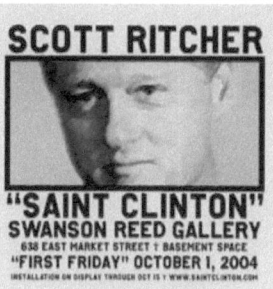

ADVERTISEMENT FOR OPENING

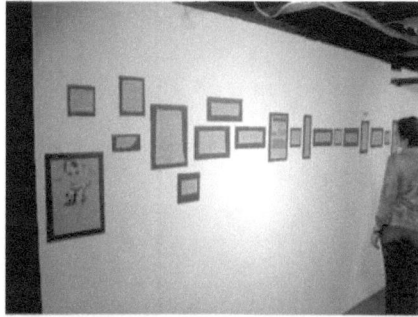

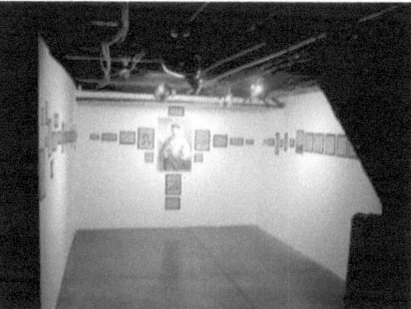

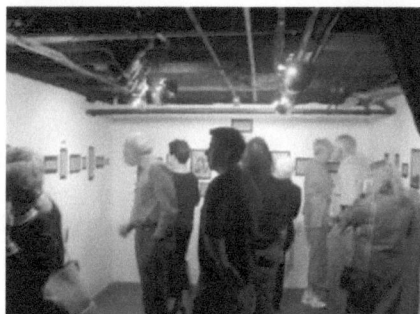

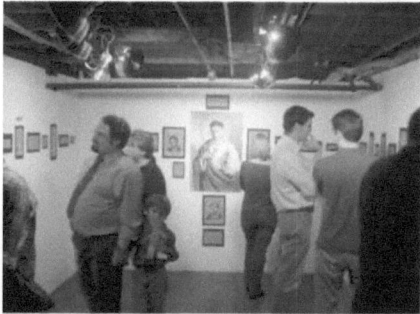

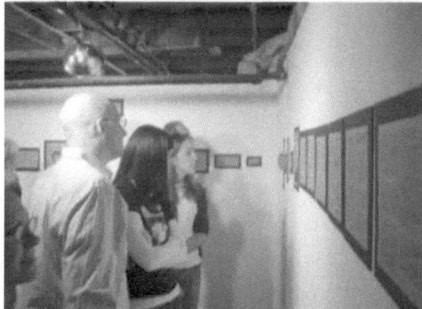

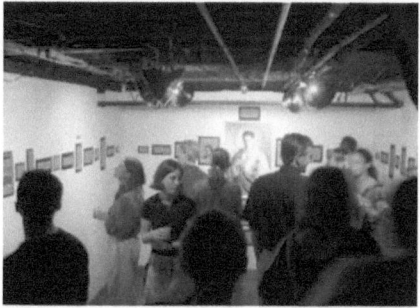

www.ingramcontent.com/pod-product-compliance
Lightning Source LLC
Chambersburg PA
CBHW020413290526
45785CB00002B/534